DISASTERS!

21 Famous Disasters—With Exercises for Developing Critical Reading Skills

Dan Dramer
Adjunct Professor of Reading/Education
Hofstra University

Jamestown Publishers
Providence, Rhode Island

Disasters!

21 Famous Disasters—With Exercises
for Developing Critical Reading Skills

Catalog No. 760

Copyright © 1982 by Jamestown Publishers

Cover and Text Design by
Deborah Hulsey Christie

Printed in the United States AL

88 89 90 9 8 7

ISBN 0-89061-247-1

Contents

Group Three

To the Teacher

Introduction

Disasters are one of our main topics of conversation. They are a major portion of the news, and they are featured by the publishing, movie and television industries. Our earliest historical records deal with floods, plagues, famines and other such misfortunes. *Disasters!* helps you capitalize on this universal fascination by using articles about disasters to guide your students in the development of their critical reading skills.

Disasters! provides interesting subject matter for thoughtful interpretation and challenges your students in four areas of critical reading: vocabulary, subject matter, important details and main idea. *Disasters!* also helps your students to improve their reading rate. The graphs at the end of the book (pages 158–159) allow students to record their progress in both comprehension and speed and they also serve as motivating devices.

Disasters! consists of twenty-one units divided into three groups of seven units each. All articles in a group are on the same reading level. Group One is at the sixth-grade reading level, Group Two is at the seventh-grade reading level, and Group Three is at the eighth-grade reading level, as assessed by the Fry Formula for Estimating Readability. Articles and questions for developing critical reading skills in students with ninth- through twelfth-grade reading levels are available in *Literary Tales*, also by Dan Dramer (Copyright © 1980 by Jamestown Publishers).

How To Use This Book

This text, used creatively, can be an effective tool for teaching critical reading skills to your students. Here are some suggestions for using this text successfully:

1. **Explain the Scorecard.** Show the Scorecard which accompanies each unit and point out the spaces for recording times and scores. Explain how the Scorecard can help the students as well as the teacher keep track of progress and discover areas which need additional work and attention. Students enjoy keeping a record of achievement and the Scorecard provides an easy and attractive means of doing this.

2. **Explain the Critical Reading Skills.** The "Developing Critical Reading Skills" section of this text (pages 8–11) contains sample passages and questions to show

students what the critical reading skills are. Read each sample passage aloud together and explain the question type that follows. Point out the directions at the beginning of each question type. Make sure that the students understand that each choice in a question is to be marked with a different letter.

3. **Introduce the Article.** Each article is accompanied by a photograph and a brief introduction to the story. Read the brief introduction aloud together; then give the students a few moments to study the photograph. Ask for their thoughts on what the article will probably be about. Continue the discussion for a minute or so.

4. **Time the Article.** Tell students the reason for timing: to record how long it takes them to read each article. The reading time is converted to a words-per-minute rate and lets students see improvement in reading speed as it occurs.

Here's one way of timing. Tell the class to begin reading. After one minute has passed, write on the chalkboard the elapsed time and begin updating it in ten-second intervals (1:00, 1:10, 1:20, *etc.*). Direct students to copy down the last time shown on the chalkboard when they have finished reading. Students then follow the instructions given in the text for converting reading times to words per minute. The conversion is entered on the Scorecard.

You may prefer to use some other method of group timing or to have students time themselves individually.

5. **Have Students Complete the Questions.** Without looking back at the article, students should go on to the four types of critical reading questions. These are the four types of questions which accompany each article:

a. *Using Words Precisely.* These questions help students build their vocabularies and also guide them in making more precise discriminations among words with similar definitions.

b. *Choosing the Best Title.* In order to choose the best title, students must have a clear grasp of the subject of the article as a whole.

c. *Recognizing Important Details.* These questions help students to focus on the details that are important while testing their ability to remember them.

d. *Finding the Main Idea.* These questions require the students to grasp the most important point in the article and to understand why other points are less central.

6. **Have Students Correct and Score Their Answers.** Using the Answer Key which starts on page 147, students can check their responses to the four types of questions. It is important for students to see what the correct response is when they have made an error. Discuss with students the proper way to score and total their scores for each type. All scores should be transferred to the Scorecard.

7. **Have Students Graph Their Work.** Working from the Scorecard, students should plot their Reading Speed and Critical Reading Score on the graphs provided at the back of the book. Explain the function of each graph fully. Discuss with students the kind of information that each graph displays. As with the questions, it may be necessary or useful to "talk students through" the plotting of times and scores for the first article to ensure that they will be using the graphs productively.

Students enjoy graphing their work.

Graphs show in a very concrete and easily understandable way the student's progress or lack of it. Seeing a connecting line of rising scores gives students the incentive to continue to strive for improvement.

8. **Check the Scorecard and Graphs Regularly.** Establish a routine for reviewing each student's progress. Discuss what you are looking for with each student and the kind of progress you expect. Establish guidelines and warning signals so that students will know when to approach the teacher for counseling and advice.

Developing Critical Reading Skills

Following each article there are four types of critical reading questions. The question types are: (1) using words precisely; (2) choosing the best title; (3) recognizing important details; and (4) finding the main idea. Each type of question will help your students develop a different reading skill. Directions preceding each question explain the method for answering the question and tell the students how to score their answers.

Question A: Using Words Precisely

This type of question tests vocabulary discrimination. The question not only helps students build their vocabularies, but it also helps them recognize precise definitions.

Five words (or phrases) from the article are used in each set of vocabulary questions. The words are quoted from the sentences in which they appear in the article. For each vocabulary word, three definitions are given. Your students pick: (1) the definition that has the *same* meaning as the vocabulary word; (2) the definition that has *almost the same* meaning; and (3) the definition *opposite* in meaning.

A sample passage and Using Words Precisely question follow. Read the sample passage and the question directions aloud with your students. Go over the three parts of the question with them and make sure they understand the answers before you go on.

Sample Passage

It was a warm summer night in 1956. The Italian liner *Andrea Doria* was on its way to New York City from Genoa, Italy, carrying 1,134 passengers. No passenger ship <u>excelled</u> the *Andrea Doria* in luxury.

A Using Words Precisely

	Answer	Score
Mark the word or phrase that has the *same* meaning as the underlined word	(S)	3
Mark the word or phrase that has *almost the same* meaning as the underlined word	(A)	1
Mark the word or phrase that is the *opposite* of the underlined word	(O)	1

		Answer	Score
1. No passenger ship excelled the *Andrea Doria* in luxury.			
	a. was inferior to	(O)	1
	b. was equal to	(A)	1
	c. was better than	(S)	3

Question B: Choosing the Best Title

The title of an article should give a clue to what the article is about without revealing too much information. The ideal title teases the reader into reading the selection because he or she wants to learn more about it. The Choosing the Best Title question tests whether your students have found out what the article is about. Three possibilities are given after each article. The students decide which one is the *best title* for the article. Then they pick the title that is *too narrow* because it tells about only one part of the article, and the title that is *too broad* because it goes beyond the topic of the article.

A sample passage and Choosing the Best Title question follow. Read the sample passage and the question instructions aloud with your students. Then go over the answers to the three parts of the question. Make sure they understand each answer before you go on to the next critical reading skill.

Sample Passage

It was a warm summer night in 1956. The Italian liner *Andrea Doria* was on its way to New York City from Genoa, Italy, carrying 1,134 passengers. No passenger ship excelled the *Andrea Doria* in luxury.

The *Doria* was about 100 miles from the United States mainland, traveling through a dense fog. It was in that busy section of the Atlantic known as "Times Square" because of the heavy ship traffic there.

One of the ships in Times Square that night was the Swedish ship *Stockholm*, outward bound from New York to her home port. The *Stockholm* therefore was heading directly toward the *Andrea Doria*.

The *Stockholm* started to steer to avoid a collision, then it suddenly turned and crashed into the *Doria*'s side.

B Choosing the Best Title

	Answer	Score
Mark the *best title*	(T)	10
Mark the title that is *too broad*	(B)	5
Mark the title that is *too narrow*	(N)	5

	Answer	Score
1. The *Andrea Doria* (This title is *too narrow*. The selection deals not just with the *Andrea Doria*, but with the *Stockholm* as well, and what happened to them.)	(N)	5
2. Luxury Liners (This title is *too broad*. A reader would expect an article with this title to be about luxury ships in general.)	(B)	5
3. Collision of the *Stockholm* and the *Andrea Doria* (This title is neither too broad nor too narrow. It gives the topic of the selection. It is the best title.)	(T)	10

Question C: Recognizing Important Details

The details of an article are its flesh and blood. Your students must learn to note important details and to remember them. The seven detail questions for each article show the students the kinds of details that are important and test their ability to remember them. The students will be asked to identify and label each detail as *true, false* or *not mentioned* in the article.

A sample passage and Recognizing Important Details question follow. Read the sample passage and the question directions with the class to make sure everyone understands how to answer the Recognizing Important Details question.

Sample Passage

There was no panic aboard the *Doria*. There was, however, a little confusion between those passengers trying to get to their staterooms below deck and those already below who were hurrying to get up on deck.

Once the passengers were on deck they scrambled into the lifeboats which had been lowered into the water. Some people climbed down rope ladders to the boats. Since the *Doria* was listing far to one side, other people were able simply to slide down the slope of the ship's side and into the boats.

The *Stockholm*, despite its bashed-in bow, was in fairly good shape. It sent out its own lifeboats and picked up 500 of the *Doria*'s survivors.

C — Recognizing Important Details

	Answer	Score
Mark the details that are *true*	(T)	5
Mark the details that are *false*	(F)	5
Mark the details that are *not mentioned* in the article	(N)	5

	Answer	Score

1. There was panic aboard the *Doria*.   **(F) 5**
   (The article states that there was *no* panic.)

2. The *Stockholm*'s captain commanded one of the lifeboats.   **(N) 5**
   (This detail is *not mentioned*.)

3. Some passengers slid down the *Doria*'s side to the lifeboats.   **(T) 5**
   (The article states that some people "were able to simply slide down ... the ship's side and into the boats.")

4. There was confusion aboard the *Doria*.   **(T) 5**
   (The article states that "there was, however, a little confusion.")

5. The lifeboats were made of varnished wood.   **(N) 5**
   (This detail is *not mentioned*.)

6. The *Stockholm* was not damaged by the crash.   **(F) 5**
   (The article states that the *Stockholm*'s bow was bashed in.)

7. At least 500 passengers on the *Doria* survived.   **(T) 5**
   (The article states that 500 of the *Doria*'s passengers were picked up by the *Stockholm*.)

Question D: Finding the Main Idea

The ability to find the main idea is fundamental to reading success. Many consider it the single most important critical reading skill. In the main idea question your students are given three statements. One of the statements is *too narrow* to be the main idea: it tells about only one part of the article. Another statement is *too broad*: it is vague and doesn't tell much about the topic of the article. The third statement is the *main idea*. It answers two questions: it tells *who* or *what* is the subject of the article, and it answers the understood question *does what?* or *is what?*

A sample passage and Finding the Main Idea question follow.

Sample Passage

The captain of the *Doria* tried to steer it away from the *Stockholm*, but there wasn't enough time. The bow of the Swedish ship had been especially reinforced for breaking through ice. Now, that icebreaker bow cut through the *Doria*'s side.

The *Stockholm* pulled back from the *Doria* leaving a jagged, forty-foot hole in the side of the Italian ship. The sea came pouring in. Everyone could see that the *Doria* had received its death blow. The *Stockholm*'s bow was torn and bent like a discarded tin can, but she was able to stay afloat.

D Finding the Main Idea

	Answer	Score
Mark the *main idea*	(M)	10
Mark the statement that is *too broad*	(B)	5
Mark the statement that is *too narrow*	(N)	5

	Answer	Score

1. The *Stockholm* cut a forty-foot hole in the *Doria*'s side.   (N) 5
   (This statement is true, but it is *too narrow*. It tells only about the extent of damage to one of the ships.)

2. There can be considerable damage when large ships collide.   (B) 5
   (This statement is *too broad*. The selection was not about large ships in general, but about what happened to the *Doria* and the *Stockholm*.)

3. The *Stockholm* was able to stay afloat after hitting the *Doria*, although the Italian ship received its death blow.   (M) 10
   (This statement gives the main idea. It answers the question *what?* by naming the *Stockholm*, the subject of the passage. It also answers the understood question *did what?* by stating that the *Stockholm* was able to stay afloat.)

To the Student

People have always been fascinated by disasters. Some of the first records that have come down to us from early times tell of floods, famines, plagues and other misfortunes. And today, we have many books, movies and TV shows about similar terrible events. *Disasters!* brings you the stories of twenty-one of the world's best-known disasters.

While you are enjoying these fascinating stories, you will be developing your reading skills. This book assumes that you already are a fairly good reader. *Disasters!* is for students who want to read faster and to increase their understanding of what they read. If you complete all twenty-one units, reading the articles and answering the questions, you will improve in both your reading rate and your comprehension.

Group One

On a quiet day in 1964, Anchorage, Alaska, was hit by an earthquake. The quake struck with a force ten million times as powerful as an atomic bomb. Streets opened—swallowed up people—and closed. The quake destroyed thirty blocks of this modern city—wiping out homes, stores and tall buildings.

Bad Good Friday in Anchorage

Read this article well enough so that you can answer questions about it. Your teacher may want you to keep track of your reading time. If so, write your reading time on the SCORECARD on page 17 after you finish the article.

Then answer the questions about the article to find out how well you understood what you read. These questions will help you sharpen your reading and thinking skills.

It was an unusually warm evening for Alaska that Good Friday of 1964. The citizens of Anchorage were looking forward to a pleasant Easter. People doing last-minute shopping for Easter finery were crowding the new J.C. Penney store. Penney's was five stories high—one of the tallest buildings in Anchorage.

At 5:36 P.M. the Penney store simply fell apart. Penney's and all of the area around Anchorage had been hit by an earthquake. The quake was ten million times as powerful as the atomic bomb that destroyed the city of Hiroshima, Japan. It measured 8.6 on the Richter scale, which measures earthquakes. (A reading of 8.5 means a violent earthquake.) The Anchorage quake was the worst in North American history.

Several other tall buildings shared the fate of the Penney store. As the *New York Times* reported, large buildings were "…shaken like a ship in a storm and crumpled like a crushed child's toy."

The quake caused slabs of concrete weighing many tons to fall from the face of the Penney building. One slab fell onto an automobile in the street below. A terrified woman in the car threw herself to its floor as the roof was squashed in and the car crushed to only three feet high. Would-be rescuers were unable to remove the concrete slab from the car's roof. They did, however, manage to cut the woman out of the car with a torch. Tragically, she died the next day from her injuries.

One man had just driven his car into the family garage when the earthquake struck. Man, car and garage were thrown through the air to land uninjured in a neighbor's yard.

Occupants of other cars did not do as well. Many cars slid into great fissures that opened in the streets. The fissures would close, crushing anything unlucky enough to be swallowed by them. Some of these cracks were twelve feet deep and fifty feet wide. Even large buildings slid into the fissures. People who streamed into the streets to escape from collapsing buildings often got caught outside. The streets rippled like waves on a body of water, as fissures continued to develop.

The earth continued to roll in wave after wave for five minutes. As the ground heaved and split open beneath people's feet, they grabbed hold of lampposts and to those buildings that were still standing Some people tried to keep on their feet and out of the fissures by clinging to each other. Some linked arms and hands to form a human chain. Some of the people forming the links in that chain had rushed out of falling buildings wearing few clothes or none at all. Everybody was too busy trying to stay alive to pay any attention to clothes.

The editor of an Anchorage newspaper ran from his home where he'd been practicing on his trumpet. He was swallowed up by a crack in the street. He felt himself grabbed and held by the soft, warm earth which lined the sides of the fissure. The editor struggled to free himself from the crack which seemed reluctant to give him up. He glanced down as he struggled and discovered that he was still holding on to his trumpet, and that the horn had become wedged between the walls of the fissure. The editor abandoned the trumpet and scrambled up the earthen sides—just as the fissure clamped closed.

The quake left nothing standing in a thirty-block downtown area. Stores, homes and offices were demolished. Part of the city had been built on a kind of soil known as Bootlegger Cove clay. The soil turned liquid and slid into the sea—carrying sections of downtown Anchorage with it.

The land at the quake's center rose more than thirty feet. The entire city of Houston, Texas, 3,300 miles from Anchorage, was lifted four inches. The sea bed of the Gulf of Alaska rose fifty feet. A giant *tsunami*, (sü-nä′-mē), a sea wave caused by an underwater earthquake, was set in motion. Waves seventeen feet high—taller than many buildings, swept ashore. These waves were felt as far away as Japan. Crescent City, California, over a thousand miles from Anchorage, was hit by five separate giant waves.

In Kodiak, Alaska, the tsunami picked up a good-sized crab-fishing boat called *The Selief*. The wave carried boat and crew inland and deposited them on the roof of a school located five blocks from the seashore.

When the tsunami hit the waterfront town of Valdez, Alaska, a father and his two small children, who were picnicing on the beach, were swept away. A pier and the twelve dock workers who were on it disappeared into the sea.

Alaska has been referred to as "the last frontier" of the United States. The citizens of Alaska are, in many ways, like pioneers, and they have the old pioneer spirit. The disaster at Valdez was so horrifying, however, that the residents left the town and never returned.

Usually major disasters have been followed by disorder and looting. Perhaps Alaska's pioneer spirit accounted for it, but there was almost no looting. The rebuilding of the northern state began almost at once. ■

Find out your reading time and enter it on the SCORECARD. Then turn to page 156 and look up your reading speed. Write the Words per Minute on the SCORECARD.

Now go on to the exercises in "How Well Did You Read?" Use the SCORECARD to record your critical reading scores. When the SCORECARD is full, transfer your Words per Minute and Critical Reading Score to the graphs on pages 158 and 159.

SCORECARD

Reading Speed

Reading Time 6 min ____ : ____

           Minutes   Seconds

Words per Minute [   ]

How Well Did You Read?

Using Words Precisely   ____

Choosing the Best Title   ____

Recognizing Important Details   ____

Finding the Main Idea   ____

Critical Reading Score [   ]
(Add the 4 scores above)

1. Bad Good Friday in Anchorage

How Well Did You Read?

Answer the four types of questions that follow. The directions for each type of question tell you how to mark and score your answers.

   After you have answered all the questions, check your work using the Answer Key on page 147. If you have the right answer, write the score on the gray line next to the answer. If your answer is wrong, write 0 on the line.

   Then add your scores for each type of question and write the total scores in the gray brackets. Enter the four total scores on the SCORECARD and add them to find your Critical Reading Score.

A   Using Words Precisely

	Answer	Score
Mark the word or phrase that has the *same* meaning as the underlined word	(S)	3
Mark the word or phrase that has *almost the same* meaning as the underlined word	(A)	1
Mark the word or phrase that is the *opposite* of the underlined word	(O)	1

		Answer	Score
1. People doing last minute shopping for Easter <u>finery</u> were crowding the new J.C. Penney store.			
	a. work clothes	(O)	____
	b. showy clothes	(A)	____
	c. dressy clothes	(S)	____
2. Many cars slid into great <u>fissures</u> that opened in the streets.			
	a. bumps	(O)	____
	b. weak spots	(A)	____
	c. breaks	(S)	____

A — Using Words Precisely (continued)

Answer   Score

3. The editor struggled to free himself from the crack which seemed <u>reluctant</u> to give him up.

   a. hesitant   (A) ___

   b. unwilling   (S) ___

   c. agreeable   (O) ___

4. Stores, homes and offices were <u>demolished</u>.

   a. damaged   (A) ___

   b. constructed   (O) ___

   c. destroyed   (S) ___

5. The wave carried boat and crew inland and <u>deposited</u> them on the roof of a school.

   a. placed   (S) ___

   b. removed   (O) ___

   c. arranged   (A) ___

Using Words Precisely Score [ ]

B — Choosing the Best Title

Answer   Score

Mark the *best title* . . . . (T) <u>10</u>

Mark the title that is *too broad* . . . . (B) <u>5</u>

Mark the title that is *too narrow* . . . . (N) <u>5</u>

Answer   Score

1. Earthquake   (B) ___

2. The Anchorage Earthquake   (T) ___

3. Waves Seventeen Feet High   (N) ___

Choosing the Best Title Score [ ]

C Recognizing Important Details

	Answer	Score
Mark the details that are *true*	(T)	5
Mark the details that are *false*	(F)	5
Mark the details that are *not mentioned* in the article	(N)	5

	Answer	Score
1. The cracks in the earth caused by the quake were barely large enough to swallow up a person.	(N)	___
2. The editor was able to use his trumpet to dig his way out of the crack in the street.	(H)	___
3. The kind of soil on which part of Anchorage was built added to the destruction of the city.	(T)	___
4. The tsunami caused high tides in New York City.	(F)	___
5. Vancouver, British Columbia, was hit by five separate giant waves.	(N)	___
6. The people of Valdez abandoned their town after the quake.	(F)	___
7. The Governor of Alaska ordered looters shot on sight.	(N)	___

Recognizing Important Details Score [ ]

D Finding the Main Idea

	Answer	Score
Mark the *main idea*	(M)	10
Mark the statement that is *too broad*	(B)	5
Mark the statement that is *too narrow*	(N)	5

	Answer	Score
1. An earthquake and tsunami struck Anchorage, Alaska, on Good Friday, 1964.		
2. The Anchorage earthquake demolished J.C. Penney's new store.		
3. Alaska has been hit by natural disasters, such as earthquakes and tsunamis.		

Finding the Main Idea Score [ ]

Tornadoes are spinning columns of air that rotate at speeds of hundreds of miles an hour. The *twisters* are whirling funnels—wide at the top, narrow at the bottom. The twister that struck St. Louis, Missouri, in 1896 was unusually destructive: the winds at its center moved at about 560 miles per hour. Here are some scenes of the destruction this tornado caused.

The Tornado That Ripped St. Louis Apart

Read this article well enough so that you can answer questions about it. Your teacher may want you to keep track of your reading time. If so, write your reading time on the SCORECARD on page 23 after you finish the article.

Then answer the questions about the article to find out how well you understood what you read. These questions will help you sharpen your reading and thinking skills.

Many of the people who lived in Missouri at the turn of the century had seen big tornadoes. Even those people who had lived through twisters of the past, however, weren't prepared for the violence of the Tornado of 1896.

The twister had given plenty of advance notice. A brilliant electrical storm struck about an hour before the tornado itself hit town. That electrical display was to continue into the next day. Forked lightning split the heavens. The low, rumbling sound of thunder never stopped. The sky turned a dirty gray color. People knew that some kind of storm was brewing. They feared, however, to use the word *tornado* in discussing the approaching weather.

Early in the evening, a storm struck, although it wasn't a tornado. There was still no sign of the swirling spout of air such as the one that carried Dorothy off to the Land of Oz. The first winds that blew over St. Louis weren't a tornado, but they did reach a speed of more than 120 miles an hour. Chimneys and telegraph poles were knocked down. The people of St. Louis thought the storm was a bad one, but they were relieved to have escaped a tornado.

Then, with a roar like the sound of a thousand express trains, the real tornado struck St. Louis.

The lightning began to flash bright green. The horrified citizens of St. Louis saw the tornado's spinning funnel bearing down on them. It looked like the swaying trunk of some great, unseen elephant.

The tornado had the strength of thousands of elephants. The force of the tornado's wind was so great that it drove wheat straws a half inch deep into living trees.

The tornado headed toward the St. Louis Fairgrounds, one of the country's most famous horse racing tracks. The last race of the day was being run when the

tornado struck. The people in the grandstands fled from their seats and headed for an open field. The roof of the grandstand blew away, killing four racing fans who weren't fast enough to get out of its way.

The twister moved over the residential part of town. It pulled the roofs off houses, sometimes replacing them with roofs that it had torn from other homes. The force of the wind was so great that twenty-five grand pianos were swirling around in the air at the same time.

The twister continued on its path of destruction. The funnel of air picked up a horse, whirled it through the air for a distance of four city blocks—and dropped it down a well. The tornado moved on and demolished the tenement district brick-by-brick.

Some of the worst damage occurred at the river front. The tornado blew the steamer *D.H. Pike* bottom side up and left it in the middle of the river. The steamer *Delaphin*, carrying twenty passengers and a crew of six sailors, was broken in two when it was slammed against the stone foundation of a bridge. Two passengers and two sailors managed to cling to the stonework of the bridge until the tornado passed.

For a time it was feared that the loss of lives aboard the many Mississippi steamers would run into the thousands. Actually, there were very few casualties aboard the steamboats. The crews of most of the boats on the river had seen the lightning and other warning signs of the approaching storm. They got the boats safely tied up at their docks before the tornado struck.

At the time when the twister hit St. Louis, the city was already the second greatest railroad center in the United States. The tornado blew away more than 500 boxcars. The twister caught a train just as it was crossing famous St. Louis's Eads Bridge, the world's finest example of metal arch construction. The twister spilled the train over onto its side. The bridge's steel wires kept the cars from being swept into the river 100 feet below. However, the train's steel and wood parts and the passengers all became twisted in those same steel wires. Rescuers worked for hours to free the passengers from the twisted mass. Amazingly, everyone in the train lived to tell of the experience.

By the time the train's last passenger was rescued, the tornado was long gone. Its trip from one end of St. Louis to the other had taken only twenty minutes. In that twenty minutes, the tornado had taken more than 300 lives and injured another 2,500 people.

St. Louis had other twisters before and has had others since, but people there will always talk of the Tornado of 1896. ■

Find out your reading time and enter it on the SCORECARD. Then turn to page 156 and look up your reading speed. Write the Words per Minute on the SCORECARD.

Now go on to the exercises in "How Well Did You Read?" Use the SCORECARD to record your critical reading scores. When the SCORECARD is full, transfer your Words per Minute and Critical Reading Score to the graphs on pages 158 and 159.

SCORECARD

Reading Speed

Reading Time _____ : _____
                  Minutes   Seconds

Words per Minute [   ]

How Well Did You Read?

Using Words Precisely _____

Choosing the Best Title _____

Recognizing Important Details _____

Finding the Main Idea _____

Critical Reading Score [   ]
(Add the 4 scores above)

**2. The Tornado That Ripped
St. Louis Apart**

How Well Did You Read?

Answer the four types of questions that follow. The directions for each type of question tell you how to mark and score your answers.

After you have answered all the questions, check your work using the Answer Key on page 147. If you have the right answer, write the score on the gray line next to the answer. If your answer is wrong, write 0 on the line.

Then add your scores for each type of question and write the total scores in the gray brackets. Enter the four total scores on the SCORECARD and add them to find your Critical Reading Score.

A — Using Words Precisely

	Answer	Score
Mark the word or phrase that has the *same* meaning as the underlined word	(S)	3
Mark the word or phrase that has *almost the same* meaning as the underlined word	(A)	1
Mark the word or phrase that is the *opposite* of the underlined word	(O)	1

	Answer	Score
1. The electrical <u>display</u> was to continue into the next day.		
a. view	(S)	____
b. exhibition	(A)	____
c. hidden sight	(O)	____
2. People knew that some sort of storm was <u>brewing</u> but they feared to use the word *tornado*.		
a. clearing up	(S)	____
b. in progress	(O)	____
c. forming	(A)	____

A Using Words Precisely (continued)

Answer   Score

3. The twister moved over the <u>residential</u> part of town.

   a. part of town where people live   (S) ____

   b. part of town where people work   (O) ____

   c. part of town that is quiet   (A) ____

4. The tornado moved on and demolished the <u>tenement district</u> brick-by-brick.

   a. wealthy section of town   (O) ____

   b. poor section of town   (A) ____

   c. old section of town   (B) ____

5. Actually, there were very few <u>casualties</u> aboard the steamboats.

   a. suffering people   (A) ____

   b. dead and injured   (S) ____

   c. unhurt survivors   (O) ____

Using Words Precisely Score [ ]

B Choosing the Best Title

Answer   Score

Mark the *best title* .... (T) <u>10</u>

Mark the title that is *too broad* .... (B) <u>5</u>

Mark the title that is *too narrow* .... (N) <u>5</u>

Answer   Score

1. Tornado Destroys St. Louis's Racetrack   (N) ____

2. St. Louis in 1896   (B) ____

3. Twister Rips St. Louis   (M) ____

Choosing the Best Title Score [ ]

C — Recognizing Important Details

	Answer	Score
Mark the details that are *true*	(**T**)	5
Mark the details that are *false*	(**F**)	5
Mark the details that are *not mentioned* in the article	(**N**)	5

	Answer	Score
1. A severe storm hit St. Louis before the tornado struck.	(T)	___
2. The force of the tornado drove straws a half foot deep into trees.	(N)	___
3. The lightning of the thunderstorm stopped before the tornado struck.	(N)	___
4. People tried to escape from the tornado by hiding in the grandstand of the track.	(F)	___
5. Most of the riverboats had been tied up before the twister struck.	(T)	___
6. The Eads Bridge had to be rebuilt after the tornado.	(N)	___
7. It took the tornado twenty minutes to cross St. Louis.	(T)	___

Recognizing Important Details Score [ ]

D — Finding the Main Idea

	Answer	Score
Mark the *main idea*	(**M**)	10
Mark the statement that is *too broad*	(**B**)	5
Mark the statement that is *too narrow*	(**N**)	5

	Answer	Score
1. A twister can be responsible for great losses of lives and of property.	(B)	___
2. An 1896 twister causes widespread destruction and loss of life in St. Louis.	(M)	___
3. The St. Louis twister was powerful enough to move a horse through the air for blocks.	(N)	___

Finding the Main Idea Score

The fire aboard the liner *Morro Castle* in 1934 is probably the most shameful story in the history of ships and the people who go to sea in them. Although it is a story filled with great cowardice, it also is a tale of great heroism.

Fire on the High Seas

4128

Read this article well enough so that you can answer questions about it. Your teacher may want you to keep track of your reading time. If so, write your reading time on the SCORECARD on page 29 after you finish the article.

Then answer the questions about the article to find out how well you understood what you read. These questions will help you sharpen your reading and thinking skills.

"What is that big ship afire off the coast at Shark River?" Several ships radioed that question to Coast Guard stations along the New Jersey coast. The Coast Guard's own shore patrols and watchtowers could see a big ship on fire only eight miles out to sea. The fire looked bad, but the ship hadn't sent an SOS or fired distress rockets.

The ship on fire was the luxury liner *Morro Castle*, completing the last part of a Havana, Cuba, to New York City trip.

The fire had begun at 3:00 A.M., just after most passengers had gone to sleep. They were tired after the traditional captain's ball, held on the last night out. Two events marred the dinner. The first spoiler was the terribly rough weather.

One-third of the passengers were seasick and had spent the whole day in bed. The second event that spoiled the captain's ball was the absence of Captain R. R. Wilmott, who had collapsed and had been carried to his cabin. During the ball it was announced that the captain had died of a heart attack.

The man who succeeded Captain Wilmott was the *Morro Castle*'s chief mate, First Officer William Warms. Warms was on watch on the bridge early in the morning of September 8, 1934. Suddenly, an alarm signaled a fire aboard the ship. Warms, as acting captain, should have issued several orders. First, he should have closed the ship's fire doors to prevent the fire from spreading. Second, he should have cut the ship's speed to prevent the wind from fanning the flames and spreading them. Then, he should have sent a radio signal that his ship was having some trouble and might need help. Acting Captain Warms did none of these things. In fact, he did just the opposite. He speeded up the *Morro Castle*. With the strong wind that was already blowing, a wind of forty knots fanned the flames. Then, Warms zig-zagged the ship, causing the wind to

spread the flames to all parts of the ship.

Junior Radio Operator George Alagna asked the captain several times for permission to send an SOS, but each time, the captain refused.

One of the junior officers, a man named Hansen, pleaded with the captain. He wanted Warms to beach the ship on the Jersey shore, only a few miles away. Warms insisted that he could make it to New York City, forty miles away. Hansen, fed up, shouted, "You damn fool.... We won't last that long." Then he punched Warms, knocking him down.

Junior Radio Operator Alagna finally wrung permission from Warms to broadcast an SOS. By this time the fire was directly under the radio shack. Alagna and Chief Radioman George White Rogers stuck to their posts, radioing for help. The heat was so intense that they had to wrap wet towels around their heads. The metal deck beneath their feet was actually glowing red, and Alagna and Rogers had to sit with their feet propped up on the rungs of their chairs.

The radio operators got off one SOS, then *Morro Castle* lost her power and the radio went dead. That single SOS was sufficient. The Coast Guard, alerted by the smoke and flames from the *Morro Castle*, already had a vessel on the way to her. They reached the ship ten minutes after receiving the SOS.

The crew was waiting for orders. Confused, Captain Warms ordered the anchor dropped and the ship swung about on her anchor chain only six miles from the big resort city of Asbury Park, New Jersey.

Chief Engineer Eban Abbot was up on deck. He phoned his engineers to stick to their posts, and most of them did. Abbot himself never showed up in the engine room. Instead, he got into the first lifeboat and ordered it to pull away from *Morro Castle*. In the boat with Abbot were thirty-one crew members and just one passenger. The loading of Abbot's boat was typical of those that left the liner. The first five boats to reach shore were half empty, holding a total of ninety-two crew members and six passengers.

The heat was intense, turning *Morro Castle* from a floating hotel to a floating crematorium. The heat and flames forced many people to jump over the ship's side. Some of them were actually on fire when they hit the water. Other people jumped because they believed that their best hope lay in swimming the six miles to shore.

Some of the lifeboats plowed right

through the midst of struggling swimmers and floating dead bodies, without stopping to pick up the swimmers. Sharks struck, adding to the horror of the situation.

The Coast Guard and a small fleet of fishing boats that had put out from shore rescued many of the swimmers. Other liners that responded to the SOS launched their lifeboats and plucked additional swimmers from the water. Despite all these heroic efforts, 134 people died—most of them passengers.

Most of the victims had burned to death within sight of the boardwalk at the Asbury Park resort. The *Morro Castle*, reduced to a burned-out hulk, drifted up on the beach just behind the Asbury Park Convention Hall.

Chief Radioman Rogers was hailed as a hero. He was the guest of parades and dinners in his honor and he was paid to go on a theater tour telling audiences of his heroic adventures.

Much later, a different picture emerged. Two books, *The Morro Castle Fire* and *Fire at Sea*, present evidence that Rogers had poisoned Captain Wilmott and started the fire. The *Morro Castle* fire was not the first fire that Rogers had been suspected of: he had been arrested for arson when he was only twelve years old. Years after the ship burned, Rogers

became involved in several murders and went to prison. His other criminal activities led many people to consider Rogers guilty of the deaths of Captain Wilmott and the other 133 victims of the *Morro Castle* fire. But Rogers's guilt has never been proven. We'll probably never know what really happened that fateful night at sea. ■

Find out your reading time and enter it on the SCORECARD. Then turn to page 156 and look up your reading speed. Write the Words per Minute on the SCORECARD.

Now go on to the exercises in "How Well Did You Read?" Use the SCORE-CARD to record your critical reading scores. When the SCORECARD is full, transfer your Words per Minute and Critical Reading Score to the graphs on pages 158 and 159.

SCORECARD

Reading Speed

Reading Time _____:_____
Minutes   Seconds

Words per Minute [   ]

How Well Did You Read?

Using Words Precisely   ——

Choosing the Best Title   ——

Recognizing Important Details   ——

Finding the Main Idea   ——

Critical Reading Score [   ]
(Add the 4 scores above)

3. Fire on the High Seas

How Well Did You Read?

Answer the four types of questions that follow. The directions for each type of question tell you how to mark and score your answers.

After you have answered all the questions, check your work using the Answer Key on page 147. If you have the right answer, write the score on the gray line next to the answer. If your answer is wrong, write 0 on the line.

Then add your scores for each type of question and write the total scores in the gray brackets. Enter the four total scores on the SCORECARD and add them to find your Critical Reading Score.

A   Using Words Precisely

	Answer	Score
Mark the word or phrase that has the *same* meaning as the underlined word	(S)	3
Mark the word or phrase that has *almost the same* meaning as the underlined word	(A)	1
Mark the word or phrase that is the *opposite* of the underlined word	(O)	1

	Answer	Score
1. Two events <u>marred</u> the dinner.		
a. made more enjoyable	(O)	——
b. spoiled	(S)	——
c. destroyed	(A)	——
2. The man who <u>succeeded</u> Captain Wilmott was the *Morro Castle*'s chief mate.		
a. took the place of	(S)	——
b. came as a result of	(A)	——
c. came before	(O)	——

A Using Words Precisely (continued)

Answer   Score

3. A junior officer wanted Warms to <u>beach</u> the ship on the Jersey shore.

    a. head out to sea   (O) ___

    b. head for port   (A) ___

    c. run the ship aground   (S) ___

4. The heat turned the *Morro Castle* from a floating hotel into a floating <u>crematorium</u>.

    a. place for dead people   (A) ___

    b. place where bodies are burned   (S) ___

    c. maternity hospital   (O) ___

5. Rogers had been arrested for <u>arson</u> when he was only twelve years old.

    a. careless handling of fire   (A) ___

    b. crime of burning up property   (S) ___

    c. extinguishing fires   (O) ___

Using Words Precisely Score [ ]

B Choosing the Best Title

Answer   Score

Mark the *best title* .... (T)   10

Mark the title that is *too broad* .... (B)   5

Mark the title that is *too narrow* .... (N)   5

Answer   Score

1. The *Morro Castle* Drifts Ashore in Asbury Park   (N) ___

2. Cruise Ship Inferno   (B) ___

3. Fatal Fire Aboard the *Morro Castle*   (T) ___

Choosing the Best Title Score [ ]

C — Recognizing Important Details

	Answer	Score
Mark the details that are *true*	(T)	5
Mark the details that are *false*	(F)	5
Mark the details that are *not mentioned* in the article	(N)	5

	Answer	Score
1. The *Morro Castle* was completing a trip from Havana, Cuba, to New Jersey.	(T)	___
2. The fire occurred during rough weather.	(T)	___
3. Captain Wilmott had had a heart attack in the past.	(N)	___
4. Warms didn't allow an SOS until just before the ship lost electrical power.	(T)	___
5. Warms hoped to tie up in New York City.	(T)	___
6. The Coast Guard had a vessel on the way before *Morro Castle* sent an SOS.	(T)	___
7. Chief Radioman Rogers was convicted of having deliberately set the *Morro Castle* on fire.	(T)	___

Recognizing Important Details Score [ ]

D — Finding the Main Idea

	Answer	Score
Mark the *main idea*	(M)	10
Mark the statement that is *too broad*	(B)	5
Mark the statement that is *too narrow*	(N)	5

	Answer	Score
1. The liner *Morro Castle* caught fire while at sea.	(M)	___
2. A total of 134 lives were lost needlessly when the *Morro Castle* burned.	(B)	___
3. When the *Morro Castle* caught fire, the captain should have cut the ship's speed.	(N)	___

Finding the Main Idea Score [ ]

Pompeii was a fashionable seaside resort in the days of the Roman emperors. Then nearby Mt. Vesuvius erupted, sending out poisonous gas that killed all living things. Vesuvius also spewed out tons of volcanic ash that formed an airtight cover over the city. Under its protective cover, Pompeii slept for 1,500 years. Today, the excavated ruins offer a glimpse of a way of life that ended 2,000 years ago.

Pompeii: The City That Slept for 1500 Years

4:41

Read this article well enough so that you can answer questions about it. Your teacher may want you to keep track of your reading time. If so, write your reading time on the SCORECARD on page 35 after you finish the article.

Then answer the questions about the article to find out how well you understood what you read. These questions will help you sharpen your reading and thinking skills.

In 1595 a worker digging a tunnel near Naples, Italy, stumbled on a buried town, but did nothing about exploring it. More than a hundred years passed before historians identified the buried town. It was Pompeii, an ancient Roman city that had been destroyed and abandoned in A.D. 79.

No attempt was made to uncover Pompeii for another half century. Then, in 1748, a Spanish Army engineer became convinced that the city held vast treasure. He obtained permission from the King of Naples to begin excavating the buried city. The excavations turned up treasure of a kind that the engineer never dreamed of.

Pompeii had been built on the slope of Mt. Vesuvius, an inactive volcano. In A.D. 79, however, Vesuvius became very active indeed. With almost no warning, there was a tremendous explosion inside the volcano.

A black cloud shaped like a pine tree formed over Vesuvius. The cloud blotted out the sun. It was as if an eclipse had come to the area. The eruption lasted seven days. Ash, stones and pieces of hardened lava spurted out of the volcano. On the seventh day, Vesuvius sent out gases that killed all living things within the volcano's reach.

The clouds of ash caused lightning storms and rain. Gradually, volcanic ash mixed with mud and rain to form a heavy paste. This paste covered the city to a depth of twelve to fifty feet. It formed a hermetically sealed layer, shutting off oxygen and preventing decay. Beneath the layer of hardened volcanic ash and mud, Pompeii lay in an unbelievably good state of preservation. It was as if the city had been frozen in place. In time, an outer layer of soil covered the layer of paste.

Nearly two thousand years later, when the city was excavated, the pictures on the walls were bright, the paint unfaded by time. Some of the food on Pompeii's tables and shelves was preserved. Stonelike loaves of petrified bread were in the ovens. Jugs still held drinkable wine. Figs, raisins and chestnuts remained in recognizable condition. Olives preserved in oil were still edible.

But the most amazing preservations were the remains of many of Pompeii's citizens. The eruption of Mt. Vesuvius had given off clouds of deadly gases. The carbon monoxide in the mixture of gases was odorless, but it was deadly. People who hadn't fled from the city died where they stood. Like their possessions, their bodies were covered and preserved by the volcanic ash and mud.

Hundreds of years after Vesuvius's eruption, excavators found the petrified body of a Roman soldier. The soldier was fully armed and standing erect. He was found at a guard post in a niche in the city wall. He had remained at his post even though a rain of ash and small stones fell from the sky.

The bodies of gladiators who were slain that day are preserved in the volcanic paste. Inside excavated temples, the petrified bodies of priests can be seen. They appear as if frozen while performing their duties.

In one home, the diggers found the stone-like remains of a man standing upright. He holds a sword in his hand, and one foot rests on a heap of gold and silver. He seems to have been protecting his wealth from looters. Near him are the bodies of five other men he struck down before he himself was struck down by Vesuvius's deadly gases. The volcanic ash preserved the looters and the guardian alike.

About 5,000 Pompeiians managed to escape the doomed city, and many more tried unsuccessfully to escape. Many tied pillows over their heads for protection against the falling stones and lava, and fled. People who left the city early enough reached the nearby Mediterranean Sea. From its shore they were able to escape in boats. Those who waited too long, however, found that wild tides had swept away the docks and boats, leaving them stranded. Others were struck down before they reached the water.

Not all the people in boats were trying to get away from Pompeii. Pliny the Elder was a famous writer as well as commander of the Roman fleet. He was about two hundred miles from Pompeii when he heard of the volcanic cloud hanging above Vesuvius. Pliny decided to investigate. He headed for Pompeii with some of his warships. As the ships approached Vesuvius, pieces of burning rock fell on the decks of the vessels. Pliny and his crew landed. They survived the falling rocks for a day, only to be killed by poisonous gas.

More than 15,000 of Pompeii's 20,000 people perished. The petrified remains of about 700 Pompeiians can be seen today. Their bodies are on display in the 160,000-acre section of the city that has been excavated.

When Pompeii was a living city, it attracted thousands of visitors. Today, the restored city attracts millions of people from all over the world. They marvel at Pompeii's preserved wonders, and, for a few hours, they step back 2,000 years to the days when Roman citizens walked the city's streets and lived in its houses. ■

Find out your reading time and enter it on the SCORECARD. Then turn to page 156 and look up your reading speed. Write the Words per Minute on the SCORECARD.

Now go on to the exercises in "How Well Did You Read?" Use the SCORECARD to record your critical reading scores. When the SCORECARD is full, transfer your Words per Minute and Critical Reading Score to the graphs on pages 158 and 159.

A money belt is still visible around the waist of this petrified body of a merchant from Pompeii.

4.40

SCORECARD

Reading Speed

Reading Time ____ : ____

Minutes   Seconds

Words per Minute [   ]

How Well Did You Read?

Using Words Precisely _____

Choosing the Best Title _____

Recognizing Important Details _____

Finding the Main Idea _____

Critical Reading Score [   ]
(Add the 4 scores above)

4. Pompeii: The City That Slept for 1500 Years

How Well Did You Read?

Answer the four types of questions that follow. The directions for each type of question tell you how to mark and score your answers.

After you have answered all the questions, check your work using the Answer Key on page 148. If you have the right answer, write the score on the gray line next to the answer. If your answer is wrong, write 0 on the line.

Then add your scores for each type of question and write the total scores in the gray brackets. Enter the four total scores on the SCORECARD and add them to find your Critical Reading Score.

A Using Words Precisely

	Answer	Score
Mark the word or phrase that has the *same* meaning as the underlined word	(S)	3
Mark the word or phrase that has *almost the same* meaning as the underlined word	(A)	1
Mark the word or phrase that is the *opposite* of the underlined word	(O)	1

	Answer	Score
1. An engineer obtained permission to begin <u>excavating</u> the buried city.		
a. burying	(O)	____
b. digging out	(S)	____
c. tunneling through	(A)	____
2. The volcanic paste formed a <u>hermetically</u> sealed layer, shutting off oxygen and preventing decay.		
a. tightly closed	(S)	____
b. airtight	(A)	____
c. exposed to oxygen	(O)	____

35

A Using Words Precisely (continued)

Answer Score

3. Stonelike loaves of <u>petrified</u> bread were in the ovens.

   a. hard   (A) ___

   b. turned to stone   (D) ___

   c. flexible   (O) ___

4. The Roman soldier was fully armed and standing <u>erect</u>.

   a. straight up   (S) ___

   b. slouched over   (O) ___

   c. tall   (A) ___

5. The soldier was found at a guard post in a <u>niche</u> in the city wall.

   a. corner angle   (O) ___

   b. spot jutting out   (A) ___

   c. hollowed-out nook   (D) ___

Using Words Precisely Score [ ]

B Choosing the Best Title

Answer Score

Mark the *best title* .... (T) <u>10</u>

Mark the title that is *too broad* .... (B) <u>5</u>

Mark the title that is *too narrow* .... (N) <u>5</u>

Answer Score

1. Vesuvius Kills 15,000   (N) ___

2. The Death and Rebirth of Pompeii   (T) ___

3. Pompeii and Vesuvius   (B) ___

Choosing the Best Title Score [ ]

C — Recognizing Important Details

	Answer	Score
Mark the details that are *true*	(T)	5
Mark the details that are *false*	(F)	5
Mark the details that are *not mentioned* in the article	(N)	5

	Answer	Score
1. The first person to discover Pompeii was looking for treasure.	(N)	___
2. Vesuvius gave frequent warnings before the big eruption that destroyed Pompeii.	(F)	___
3. Some of the pictures on the wall of Pompeii's buildings were by famous artists.	(N)	___
4. Some of Pompeii's wines were still drinkable over a thousand years later.	(T)	___
5. Roman soldiers were guarding Pompeii when Vesuvius erupted.	(T)	___
6. Pliny was in Pompeii when Vesuvius erupted.	(F)	___
7. The preserved remains of 15,000 Pompeiians can be seen today.	(F)	___

Recognizing Important Details Score [ ]

D — Finding the Main Idea

	Answer	Score
Mark the *main idea*	(M)	10
Mark the statement that is *too broad*	(B)	5
Mark the statement that is *too narrow*	(N)	5

	Answer	Score
1. A volcanic eruption can preserve an ancient city.	(N)	___
2. Mt. Vesuvius erupted, killing thousands of citizens of Pompeii.	(B)	___
3. A volcanic eruption destroyed Pompeii, but also preserved it.	(M)	___

Finding the Main Idea Score [ ]

Coal mining is one of the world's most dangerous jobs. The miners at the Monongah mine in West Virginia knew of the danger, but went down into the mine, anyway. Almost 400 of them were deep in the mine when it exploded in a blast that rattled windows six miles away. This photograph shows part of the collapsed mine the day after the explosion.

5

Monongah Mine Explosion Traps 368

4i5l

Read this article well enough so that you can answer questions about it. Your teacher may want you to keep track of your reading time. If so, write your reading time on the SCORECARD on page 41 after you finish the article.

Then answer the questions about the article to find out how well you understood what you read. These questions will help you sharpen your reading and thinking skills.

On the morning of December 6, 1907, the *fire bosses* (inspectors) at the Monongah, West Virginia, coal mine made a thorough inspection for methane. They found no trace of the deadly gas that makes coal mining so dangerous. *Fire damp*, or methane, to use the gas's scientific name, is not only suffocating, but also highly explosive. Miners have feared it since people first dug into the earth for coal.

In past times, miners brought canaries into mines to detect *fire damp*. The birds are so sensitive to *fire damp* that they fall unconscious and even die in the presence of the gas. When this happened, the miners either left the mine or used fans to ventilate the mine and drive off the gas.

The inspectors at the Monongah mine used the latest equipment to test for *fire damp*, but they found none.

The mine had a twenty-two foot fan at the mouth of the mine shaft, the largest ventilator in use in any mine in the United States. Although the miners still worked by the light of open-flame lanterns attached to their hardhats, the giant fan was run by an electric motor. Electricity was also used for pumping water out of the mine, cutting in the seam of coal, and for running the train of cars used for hauling coal to the surface.

On December 6, 1907, an eighteen-year old miner was running the eighteen-car electric train. As the cars reached the top of the incline, a pin that held two of the cars together snapped off, causing the train to start to roll back. The miner who was operating the train ran ahead of it in an effort to cut off the electricity before the cars reached the bottom. The train's rate of descent was too fast for the miner, however, and the cars slammed into a wall, cutting the electric cables that ran along it.

The sparks from the broken wires touched off the *fire damp*, which, in turn, detonated the highly-explosive coal dust that filled the air of the mine.

The boom rattled windows six miles away.

The operator of the train of cars survived, after being blown straight back and out of the mouth of the mine. But 362 other people in the Monongah mine were not so lucky.

The Monongah mine was a network of mineshafts and tunnels that honeycombed the West Virginia Hills. The two mines involved in the explosion, Number Six and Number Eight, were connected underground, although their entrance shafts came up on opposite sides of the South Fork River. The explosion had completely blown out the entrance to Number Six, sealing it with tons of earth, rock and coal. The entrances of Number Eight were still open, however.

Just about everyone in the town of Monongah had relatives working in the mine. The townspeople rushed to the mine at the first sound of the explosion. They found clouds of smoke and dust pouring from the entrance of Number Eight. Many of the townspeople who had gathered at the entrance swore they could see miners staggering from the shaft, but, unfortunately, these miners were alive only in the imaginations and wishful thinking of their friends and relatives. Nothing really came out of the mine entrance but large amounts of *fire damp*. The gas was so deadly that it withered the grass and shrubs around the mine entrance.

The rescue crews were handicapped by the *fire damp* which made it all but impossible for them to breathe. At the end of twenty-four days, rescuers had recovered 362 bodies—many of them torn and blackened by the explosion. The dead included visitors to the mine, some mine company managers and a group of twelve-year-old apprentice miners. One of the corpses belonged to an insurance company representative who had gone into the mine to sell the miners insurance. Little did he—or they—know how much they needed insurance.

Of the 368 people who had been in the mine when it blew up, only six survived. One of the survivors was Peter Urban, who had come to West Virginia from Poland. Urban had been in a side tunnel near the mouth of the mine at the time of the explosion. A rescue crew found him unconscious but alive. Unfortunately,

Urban's reprieve from death in the Monongah mine did not last. He returned to the mine and was killed twenty years later when it caved in. ■

Find out your reading time and enter it on the SCORECARD. Then turn to page 156 and look up your reading speed. Write the Words per Minute on the SCORECARD.

Now go on to the exercises in "How Well Did You Read?" Use the SCORE-CARD to record your critical reading scores. When the SCORECARD is full, transfer your Words per Minute and Critical Reading Score to the graphs on pages 158 and 159.

SCORECARD

Reading Speed

Reading Time _____ : _____
Minutes   Seconds

Words per Minute [   ]

How Well Did You Read?

Using Words Precisely _____

Choosing the Best Title _____

Recognizing Important Details _____

Finding the Main Idea _____

Critical Reading Score [   ]
(Add the 4 scores above)

5. Monongah Mine Explosion Traps 368

How Well Did You Read?

Answer the four types of questions that follow. The directions for each type of question tell you how to mark and score your answers.

After you have answered all the questions, check your work using the Answer Key on page 148. If you have the right answer, write the score on the gray line next to the answer. If your answer is wrong, write 0 on the line.

Then add your scores for each type of question and write the total scores in the gray brackets. Enter the four total scores on the SCORECARD and add them to find your Critical Reading Score.

A — Using Words Precisely

	Answer	Score
Mark the word or phrase that has the *same* meaning as the underlined word	(S)	3
Mark the word or phrase that has *almost the same* meaning as the underlined word	(A)	1
Mark the word or phrase that is the *opposite* of the underlined word	(O)	1

	Answer	Score
1. In past times, miners brought canaries into the mine to <u>detect</u> *fire damp.*		
a. notice	(A)	_____
b. discover	(S)	_____
c. hide	(O)	_____
2. As the cars reached the top of the <u>incline</u>, a pin that held two of the cars together snapped off.		
a. slope	(S)	_____
b. bend	(A)	_____
c. flat place	(O)	_____

A — Using Words Precisely (continued)

Answer   Score

3. The train's rate of <u>descent</u> was too fast for the miner.

    a. climbing   (O) ___

    b. moving   (A) ___

    c. going down   (S) ___

4. Sparks touched off the *fire damp* which, in turn, <u>detonated</u> the highly explosive coal dust in the mine.

    a. calmed down   (O) ___

    b. blew up   (D) ___

    c. set on fire   (A) ___

5. Unfortunately, Urban's <u>reprieve</u> from death did not last.

    a. temporary relief   (P) ___

    b. sentence   (A) ___

    c. permanent freedom   (D) ___

Using Words Precisely Score [ ]

B — Choosing the Best Title

Answer   Score

Mark the *best title* .... (T)   10

Mark the title that is *too broad* .... (B)   5

Mark the title that is *too narrow* .... (N)   5

Answer   Score

1. Deadly *Fire Damp*   (B) ___

2. Dangers of Coal Mining   (H) ___

3. Coal Mine Explosion   (N) ___

Choosing the Best Title Score [ ]

C   Recognizing Important Details

	Answer	Score
Mark the details that are *true*	(T)	5
Mark the details that are *false*	(F)	5
Mark the details that are *not mentioned* in the article	(N)	5

	Answer	Score
1. The mine had been found free of coal damp shortly before it blew up.	(T)	___
2. The *fire bosses* used a live canary to test for gas.	(T)	___
3. The operator of the train managed to turn off the electricity just before the train crashed.	(F)	___
4. The train operator was killed in the mine blast.	(F)	___
5. A bridge spanned the South Fork River, connecting mines on both sides of the river.	(T)	___
6. The president of the mining company was injured in the explosion.	(N)	___
7. One of the survivors of the explosion was killed in a later disaster at the same mine.	(T)	___

Recognizing Important Details Score [ ]

D   Finding the Main Idea

	Answer	Score
Mark the *main idea*	(M)	10
Mark the statement that is *too broad*	(B)	5
Mark the statement that is *too narrow*	(N)	5

	Answer	Score
1. The Monongah mine explosion withered nearby grass and shrubs.	(N)	___
2. Explosions and cave-ins make coal mining a dangerous occupation.	(M)	___
3. A *fire damp* explosion cost the lives of 362 people in Monongah, West Virginia.	(B)	___

Finding the Main Idea Score [ ]

In the 1930s, many thought that the future of air travel rested with the zeppelin. There was only one problem: dirigibles were kept in the air by hydrogen—a highly flammable, explosive gas. In 1937, the German zeppelin *Hindenburg* blew up in the United States. What caused the explosion? Was it an electric spark? Sabotage? Static electricity? Investigators are still puzzled.

The *Hindenburg:*
Last of the Great Dirigibles

Read this article well enough so that you can answer questions about it. Your teacher may want you to keep track of your reading time. If so, write your reading time on the SCORECARD on page 47 after you finish the article.

Then answer the questions about the article to find out how well you understood what you read. These questions will help you sharpen your reading and thinking skills.

The *Hindenburg* was a big, modern and powerful airship. To the people of Germany, the huge dirigible was a proud symbol of the German nation itself. To Adolf Hitler, it was the showpiece of the new Germany rebuilding itself after its defeat in the first World War.

Germany had every reason to be proud of the *Hindenburg*. It was the largest airship ever built. The great silver liner was more than three blocks long. It measured 804 feet from nose to rudder, marked with huge, black Nazi swastikas. Since the *Hindenburg's* launching in 1936 it had completed thirty-seven ocean crossings.

On this crossing in May, 1937, the *Hindenburg* was carrying a crew of sixty-one plus ninety-seven passengers. The passengers had paid $400, a great deal of money in those days, for the three-day trip. Their $400 let them travel in great comfort and luxury. Dinner included such delicacies as lobster. The list of wines the *Hindenburg* carried was more than a page long. No possible item for the passengers' comfort or safety had been overlooked.

Passengers had to give up their own matches and cigarettes when they came aboard the airship. The *Hindenburg's* great silver gasbag was filled with hydrogen, a highly flammable gas. The crew was taking no chances. To prevent accidental fire, smoking was permitted only in one completely fireproof room. Metal ladders and railings were encased in rubber to prevent sparks. These precautions resulted in an enviable safety record. No accident had occurred in fourteen years of commercial dirigible flights.

This flight had started without a hitch. The *Hindenburg* was, however, several hours behind schedule after bucking strong headwinds over the Atlantic. In addition, mooring (tying the airship to a mast) was being delayed by heavy rain. Despite weather conditions, the *Hindenburg* had already passed over New York City and was approaching Lakehurst, about sixty miles from New York City. The *Hindenburg* had tied up at Lakehurst on all previous flights to the United States, and the navy was waiting for it on this trip. Dozens of marines and sailors were on hand to pull in the mooring lines let down from the zeppelin. These long ropes would hold it down until its nose could be secured to the mooring mast.

As the airship settled gracefully to the ground, the Lakehurst crew moved forward. Waiting behind them were more than a thousand spectators who had come, despite the rain, to watch the *Hindenburg* moor. The crowd included newspaper and movie photographers, reporters and the friends and relatives of arriving passengers. They all watched the airship float down like a feather.

Boom!

There was a dull explosion and a flash of light from near the *Hindenburg's* tail. In seconds, the airship had become a great, flaming torch. The great black swastikas on its tail disappeared in flames. The flaming zeppelin slowly settled to the ground. Members of the ground crew scrambled for their lives. Flaming pieces of the *Hindenburg's* fabric covering fluttered to the ground among the navy men still below the dirigible as it continued its descent.

One passenger, Joseph Spahs, an acrobat, leaped to the ground from an open window. He landed unburned and completely unhurt. Other passengers and crew members also leaped from the flaming dirigible and lived. Some, however, were killed by the fall. Others survived the jump only to die later from burns suffered before they leaped.

Sailors and marines who had fled from the downward path of the fiery dirigible returned heroically to the airship to pull people from the flaming wreckage. These sailors and marines are credited with saving many lives. One passenger, his clothes completely burned off, was met by the navy men as he walked away from the flames. "I'm completely all right," he said. Then he dropped dead.

The *Hindenburg's* two captains, Ernst Lehmann and Max Pruss, were the last to jump from the flaming wreckage. The *Hindenburg* had had two captains on its fateful trip. Captain Lehmann had commanded the airship on its first voyages. Captain Pruss was in command during this last flight. The hair and clothing of both men were aflame as they left the dirigible's control car. Captain Pruss, though badly burned, lived. Captain Lehmann was not as lucky. Lehmann had been a dirigible pioneer. He had commanded the German zeppelins that had bombed London during the first World War. Now, the terribly burned Lehmann kept repeating, "I shall live. I shall live."

Despite his statement, Captain Lehmann died within twenty-four hours. The captain did live long enough, however, to offer his view that the explosion had been caused by sabotage—by a deliberately placed bomb.

People still speculate about the cause of the explosion. The official explanation of the Zeppelin Transport Company, which operated the airship, is that static electricity caused by the rainstorm ignited the explosive hydrogen.

One member of the United States ground crew had a different explanation. He saw a ripple—a sort of flutter—in the fabric near the *Hindenburg's* tail. That flutter may have been caused by escaping hydrogen gas as it passed over the zeppelin's skin. Then, when the engines were thrown into reverse to assist in the landing, sparks were thrown off. Several observers saw sparks that could easily have ignited the flammable gas.

What really caused the explosion? Was it escaping hydrogen? Sabotage? Static electricity? We will probably never know the truth. One terrible truth is known; the end of the *Hindenburg* brought an end to the lives of thirty-six people. It also brought to an end the age of the giant dirigibles. ∎

Find out your reading time and enter it on the SCORECARD. Then turn to page 156 and look up your reading speed. Write the Words per Minute on the SCORECARD.

Now go on to the exercises in "How Well Did You Read?" Use the SCORE-CARD to record your critical reading scores. When the SCORECARD is full, transfer your Words per Minute and Critical Reading Score to the graphs on pages 158 and 159.

SCORECARD

Reading Speed

Reading Time _____ : _____
Minutes   Seconds

Words per Minute [   ]

How Well Did You Read?

Using Words Precisely _____

Choosing the Best Title _____

Recognizing Important Details _____

Finding the Main Idea _____

Critical Reading Score [   ]
(Add the 4 scores above)

6. The *Hindenburg*: Last of the Great Dirigibles

How Well Did You Read?

Answer the four types of questions that follow. The directions for each type of question tell you how to mark and score your answers.

After you have answered all the questions, check your work using the Answer Key on page 148. If you have the right answer, write the score on the gray line next to the answer. If your answer is wrong, write 0 on the line.

Then add your scores for each type of question and write the total scores in the gray brackets. Enter the four total scores on the SCORECARD and add them to find your Critical Reading Score.

A Using Words Precisely

	Answer	Score
Mark the word or phrase that has the *same* meaning as the underlined word	(S)	3
Mark the word or phrase that has *almost the same* meaning as the underlined word	(A)	1
Mark the word or phrase that is the *opposite* of the underlined word	(O)	1

	Answer	Score
1. The *Hindenburg* measured 804 feet from nose to <u>rudder</u>.		
a. end	(A)	____
b. tail fin	(S)	____
c. bow	(O)	____
2. Lehmann had been a dirigible <u>pioneer</u>.		
a. a person who does something last	(O)	____
b. a person who does something bravely	(S)	____
c. a person who does something first	(A)	____

A Using Words Precisely (continued)

Answer Score

3. Long ropes would hold the *Hindenburg* down until it could be <u>secured</u> to the mooring mast.

   a. freed to move   (O) ___

   b. tied loosely   (A) ___

   c. firmly fastened   (S) ___

4. Flaming pieces of the *Hindenburg*'s fabric covering <u>fluttered</u> to the ground.

   a. moved slowly and smoothly   (S) ___

   b. moved rapidly and irregularly   (D) ___

   c. moved in circles   (A) ___

5. People still <u>speculate</u> about the cause of the explosion.

   a. think about   (S) ___

   b. refuse to consider   (O) ___

   c. form theories about   (A) ___

Using Words Precisely Score [ ]

B Choosing the Best Title

Answer Score

Mark the *best title* . . . . (T) <u>10</u>

Mark the title that is *too broad* . . . . (B) <u>5</u>

Mark the title that is *too narrow* . . . . (N) <u>5</u>

Answer Score

1. A German/United States Tragedy   (B) ___

2. Explosion of the *Hindenburg*   (T) ___

3. Thirty-Six Passengers Die   (N) ___

Choosing the Best Title Score [ ]

C — Recognizing Important Details

	Answer	Score
Mark the details that are *true*	(**T**)	5
Mark the details that are *false*	(**F**)	5
Mark the details that are *not mentioned* in the article	(**N**)	5

		Answer	Score
1.	The *Hindenburg* had already crossed the ocean thirty-seven times.	(F)	___
2.	Smoking was absolutely forbidden aboard the *Hindenburg*.	(F)	___
3.	The crew of the *Hindenburg* wore non-flammable uniforms.	(N)	___
4.	The *Hindenburg* had been delayed by bad weather.	(T)	___
5.	Because it represented a fire hazard, the *Hindenburg* was forbidden to fly over New York City.	(N)	___
6.	Captain Pruss's wife was among the people waiting for the *Hindenburg* to land at Lakehurst.	(N)	___
7.	The Zeppelin Transport Company believed that the *Hindenburg* was the victim of sabotage.	(M)	___

Recognizing Important Details Score [ ]

D — Finding the Main Idea

	Answer	Score
Mark the *main idea*	(**M**)	10
Mark the statement that is *too broad*	(**B**)	5
Mark the statement that is *too narrow*	(**N**)	5

		Answer	Score
1.	The *Hindenburg*'s explosion ended thirty-six lives and the commercial use of the dirigible.	(M)	___
2.	The pride of Germany went down in the *Hindenburg*'s flames.	(B)	___
3.	The black swastika on the *Hindenburg*'s rudder disappeared first in the flames.	(N)	___

Finding the Main Idea Score [ ]

Take to the Hills!
The Johnstown Dam Is Going!

Read this article well enough so that you can answer questions about it. Your teacher may want you to keep track of your reading time. If so, write your reading time on the SCORECARD on page 53 after you finish the article.

Then answer the questions about the article to find out how well you understood what you read. These questions will help you sharpen your reading and thinking skills.

The rider galloped at top speed down the hill and on into the valley, through the pouring rain. "The dam is going!" A few residents of Johnstown, Pennsylvania, took the rider's advice—and lived. Thousands of people, however, either never got the rider's message or chose to disregard it. Many of those who didn't heed the warning paid with their lives.

The citizens of Johnstown in 1889 had good reason for ignoring the advice. Once a year the old South Fork Dam seemed about to burst. The cry, "Take to the hills," had become an annual false alarm.

This time, however, the rider who carried the warning should have been taken in earnest. The rider was John G. Parke, a civil engineer who was in charge of the dam.

The Great South Fork Dam was a huge earthen dike holding the waters of an artificial lake. The dam had been constructed without any stone or cement. It had been built by piling layer upon layer of soil, until the dam was 100 feet high. It was 90 feet wide at the base.

The dam had passed through the hands of a series of owners. In recent years the dam and the lake behind it had been bought by a group of millionaires. The millionaires called themselves the Great South Fork Fishing and Hunting Club. They spent thousands of dollars stocking the lake with fish. They also added screens to prevent the fish from getting out through the dam's drainage holes.

Fishing was good and the lake had never been higher than that spring of 1889. May had been an unusually rainy month. The streets in the lower parts of Johnstown were already flooded with six feet of water. Behind the dam, the lake had been rising at the rate of one foot per hour. The owners of the fishing club sent workers to pile more dirt on top of the dam to keep it from overflowing. The owners also ordered the workers to remove the screens which had become jammed with fish, sticks and other debris. The workers tried hard to clear the jam, but John Parke's trained engineer's eye could see that their efforts would be useless. Parke saddled a horse and began his Paul Revere ride through the valley.

The rain continued to pour. At noon, the water washed over the top of the dam. Almost immediately a big notch developed in the top of the dike. Then, according to witnesses, the whole dam simply disappeared. One minute there was a dam—the next minute, nothing. The lake moved into the valley like a living thing. In little more than half an hour, the dam emptied completely, sending 4.5 *billion* gallons of water down the valley toward Johnstown. A wave of water reaching 125 feet high raced toward the city, leaping forward at the rate of 22 feet per second.

The huge wall of water approached East Conemaugh, a suburb of Johnstown. As it did, railroad engineer John Hess looked up from the string of freight cars his locomotive was pushing. He saw the water bearing down on him, now moving at fifty miles per hour. Hess moved the locomotive's throttle to wide open. Still

In 1889 the old South Fork Dam burst, sending a wave 125 feet high crashing towards Johnstown, Pennsylvania. Those who weren't killed by the mountain of water died in the fire that engulfed the floating wreckage of their homes.

pushing a string of freight cars before him, he raced the advancing flood into East Conemaugh. Hess tied down the locomotive's whistle and its screaming blast preceded the train into the village. Johnstown was a railroad city. People in the whole Johnstown area knew that a tied-down whistle could only mean a disaster. And the already flooded streets told them what kind of disaster it was. Many people who had ignored earlier warnings now headed for the hills. Unable to reach the center of Johnstown, Railroader Hess jumped from the locomotive cab in East Conemaugh, ran into his house, and roused his family. The Hesses made their way up the side of a hill just before the flood hit the village.

As the great tumbling hill of water roared on toward the center of Johnstown, it ran into the East Conemaugh rail yard. In the yard was a roundhouse containing thirty-seven locomotives. The onrushing flood swept away both roundhouse and engines. The rush of waters was so forceful that it carried the locomotives, weighing forty tons each, on top of the flood.

The rolling mountain of water, now filled with locomotives, freight cars, houses, trees, horses and humans, rushed on. A great cloud of dust and moisture rolled before the racing flood waters. The dust cloud was so heavy that many residents of Johnstown never saw the rolling flood waters behind it. The cloud was quickly named the *death mist*.

The mountain of water continued its headlong rush. Just before it reached Johnstown, it destroyed the Gautier Wire Works. The buildings of the wire works and its hundreds of miles of flesh-piercing barbed wire were added to the swirling debris.

The giant rolling hill of water rushed into the heart of Johnstown. The flood swept into two distinct parts like the arms of the letter *Y*. One arm of the flood roared through the residential part of town. Churches, schools and houses gave way before its power; 800 homes were flushed away.

The second arm of the flood, a tumbling mass of houses, trains, people and animals, swept up to a stone bridge that spanned the valley. The debris caught in the bridge's stone arches and became wedged there. A collection of hundreds of parts of buildings and thousands of people became hopelessly bound in coils of barbed wire. The water formed a great swirling whirlpool behind them. Hundreds of additional people had approached the whirlpool on makeshift rafts made from pieces of wreckage. They leaped onto the swirling debris, joining the people already trapped there.

Now a new horror broke out. Many stoves, their fires still burning, floated into and ignited the mass of debris. People on the bridge overhead and on the nearby shore managed to rescue some people by reaching for them with long poles and ropes. Thousands of victims found themselves trapped between the still rising water and the flames. Some accounts of the flood claim that 200 victims committed suicide by deliberately jumping into the flames. They were just a few of the 2,000 to 7,000 people believed to have lost their lives at Johnstown.

A week after the flood, a demolitions expert placed nine fifty-pound cases of dynamite in the debris and cleared the jam. The waters were free to pass under the bridge and continue the seventy-five mile trip down the valley to Pittsburgh. The people of that city made an astonishing find. The flood waters had carried a piece of wooden flooring from Johnstown to Pittsburgh. On that bit of wreckage, completely unhurt by the wild ride, was a healthy five-month-old baby. ■

Find out your reading time and enter it on the SCORECARD. Then turn to page 156 and look up your reading speed. Write the Words per Minute on the SCORECARD.

Now go on to the exercises in "How Well Did You Read?" Use the SCORECARD to record your critical reading scores. When the SCORECARD is full, transfer your Words per Minute and Critical Reading Score to the graphs on pages 158 and 159.

How Well Did You Read?

Answer the four types of questions that follow. The directions for each type of question tell you how to mark and score your answers.

After you have answered all the questions, check your work using the Answer Key on page 149. If you have the right answer, write the score on the gray line next to the answer. If your answer is wrong, write 0 on the line.

Then add your scores for each type of question and write the total scores in the gray brackets. Enter the four total scores on the SCORECARD and add them to find your Critical Reading Score.

A   Using Words Precisely

	Answer	Score
Mark the word or phrase that has the *same* meaning as the underlined word	(S)	3
Mark the word or phrase that has *almost the same* meaning as the underlined word ...	(A)	1
Mark the word or phrase that is the *opposite* of the underlined word	(O)	1

	Answer	Score

1. This time, the rider who carried the warning should have been taken in <u>earnest</u>.

   a. with few doubts   (A) _____

   b. seriously   (S) _____

   c. lightly   (O) _____

2. Thousands of people chose to <u>disregard</u> the message.

   a. heed   (O) _____

   b. forget   (A) _____

   c. ignore   (S) _____

53

A — Using Words Precisely (continued)

Answer   Score

3. The owners ordered the workers to <u>remove</u> the screens which had become jammed.

    a. take off   (S) ___

    b. move over   (A) ___

    c. put on   (O) ___

4. The engineer could see that the workers' efforts would be <u>useless</u>.

    a. with results   (A) ___

    b. without profit   (O) ___

    c. without success   (S) ___

5. John Parke's <u>trained</u> engineer's eye could see that the situation was serious.

    a. smart   (A) ___

    b. unskilled   (O) ___

    c. educated   (S) ___

Using Words Precisely Score   [ ]

B — Choosing the Best Title

Answer   Score

Mark the *best title* .... (**T**)   <u>10</u>

Mark the title that is *too broad* .... (**B**)   <u>5</u>

Mark the title that is *too narrow* .... (**N**)   <u>5</u>

Answer   Score

1. Johnstown, Pennsylvania   (B) ___

2. The Johnstown Flood   (T) ___

3. The Great South Fork Dam   (N) ___

Choosing the Best Title Score   [ ]

C   Recognizing Important Details

	Answer	Score
Mark the details that are *true*	(T)	5
Mark the details that are *false*	(F)	5
Mark the details that are *not mentioned* in the article	(N)	5

	Answer	Score
1. The people of Johnstown had been told in the past that the dam was bursting.	(T)	___
2. The Mayor of Johnstown believed John Parke, and left town with his family.	(N)	___
3. The South Fork Dam had been built by a group of millionaires.	(T)	___
4. Many of the millionaires of the Great South Fork Fishing and Hunting Club lost their lives in the flood.	(N)	___
5. Johnstown's streets were deep in water even before the dam burst.	(F)	___
6. A dust cloud prevented many people from seeing the rushing water.	(T)	___
7. The jam at the stone bridge was broken up by dynamiting the bridge.	(T)	___

Recognizing Important Details Score [ ]

D   Finding the Main Idea

	Answer	Score
Mark the *main idea*	(M)	10
Mark the statement that is *too broad*	(B)	5
Mark the statement that is *too narrow*	(N)	5

	Answer	Score
1. Some people tried to escape the Johnstown flood by making rafts from the wreckage.	(N)	___
2. Johnstown was destroyed by a flood released when a dam gave way.	(M)	___
3. The tragedy at Johnstown resulted from a combination of human error and natural causes.	(B)	___

Finding the Main Idea Score [ ]

Group Two

"God Himself couldn't sink the *Titanic*," somebody said. Yet sink it did—and before it had completed its first trip. The *Titanic* carried over 1,500 people with it to a watery grave. As the ship sank, the gallant band played ragtime, then switched to a hymn. Pictured below (inset) is the midget sub *Alvin*, used in 1985 to discover and photograph the *Titanic* in her resting place two and a half miles below the ocean's surface.

8

Death of the Unsinkable *Titanic*

Read this article well enough so that you can answer questions about it. Your teacher may want you to keep track of your reading time. If so, write your reading time on the SCORE-CARD on page 61 after you finish the article.

Then answer the questions about the article to find out how well you understood what you read. These questions will help you sharpen your reading and thinking skills.

"The safest ship afloat. A sea-going hotel! Unsinkable!" These were the words the newspapers used in writing about the *Titanic*, the largest ship ever built.

The year was 1912. The *Titanic* was on her first trip. She was sailing from Southampton, England, to New York City. She was captained by E. C. Smith, a veteran of many years of transatlantic service. Smith wanted to prove that the *Titanic* was not only the world's most luxurious ship, but the fastest as well. Smith held the *Titanic* to twenty-two knots for most of the voyage.

The *Titanic* carried the very latest in wireless equipment. She received messages from two nearby ships. They warned that they had seen many icebergs. In spite of the warnings, the *Titanic* continued at twenty-two knots.

Lookout Fred Fleet peered ahead from his position high up on the mast. He could see a huge bulk looming in the *Titanic*'s path. Iceberg! Fleet struck three bells—the signal for something dead ahead. First Officer Murdoch, on watch on the bridge, ordered *hard-a-starboard*. Amost at the same instant, Murdoch signaled the engine room to stop. The *Titanic* turned to one side, seeming to take forever. Too late! With a long, grinding sound, the *Titanic* scraped along the side of the iceberg. The passengers felt almost no shock. The blow was a glancing one; it was almost a near miss. Pieces of ice rained down on one of the *Titanic*'s decks. The passengers, in a holiday mood, felt no sense of danger. After all, everyone knew the *Titanic* was unsinkable. Besides, the crash had been a mere scrape. Card players continued their games. Some passengers sent waiters to pick up chunks of ice from the deck. They used the ice to cool their drinks.

Down in the engine room, the crew could see that the *Titanic*'s hurt was serious. The berg had ripped a long, jagged gash below the vessel's waterline. The sea was pouring in.

The *Titanic* had compartments that divided her into sections from bow to stern. She had been designed so that if any compartment were holed, watertight doors could shut off that section. The undamaged compartments would be more than enough to keep the ship afloat. If the *Titanic* had struck the iceberg head on, damage would have been much less. At worst, the bow and the first couple of watertight compartments would have been damaged. When the *Titanic* turned to avoid the berg, however, her hull scraped along the berg. A jagged underwater spur of ice had slashed a three-hundred foot wound in the *Titanic*'s side. Water was pouring into too many of the watertight sections.

In ten minutes, the water in the forward part of the ship was eight feet deep. Though the ship's pumps had been started up, they were of little help. Below in the firerooms, half-naked, sweating stokers shoveled coal. They fed the great furnaces of the *Titanic*'s boilers. Those boilers supplied power for the pumps, and provided electricity for the lights and the wireless.

The engineers and stokers were fighting a losing battle. Water was flooding in much too fast for the pumps. Slowly, the engine room crew retreated before the advancing water. Many of the boilers were flooded out. Enough, however, kept working to furnish electricity for the lights and the wireless.

The *Carpathia*, hours away, heard the

Titanic's SOS. The *Carpathia* doubled the number of stokers feeding her furnaces. She sent a wireless message to the *Titanic:* "Coming hard!"

Titanic's captain gave the order to abandon ship. The old rule of the sea—women and children first—was sounded. Not many passengers responded to it. People simply would not believe that the *Titanic,* with her double bottom and watertight compartments, could sink. Many women refused to be parted from their husbands. The first lifeboats pulled away from the ship only half filled.

The sinking *Titanic* was bathed in the glow of distress rockets that she fired every few minutes. Passengers began to understand that the impossible was actually happening. The *Titanic* was going down! Now the boats were more heavily loaded. People began to realize there would be not nearly enough room in the boats for all of them. They began to panic. Now the *Titanic's* bow was deep under water. Her stern rose in the air. Finally, her screws—those gigantic propellers that had driven her toward a new speed record and toward disaster—were swinging up. Finally they were completely out of the water.

People in the lifeboats could see, by the glare of the *Titanic's* lights, the hundreds of passengers left to their fate aboard the ship. The occupants of the boats watched with a grim fascination. They could see their doomed husbands, relatives, and friends aboard the now rapidly sinking ship. With a great final shudder, the *Titanic* stood on end. Then she plunged beneath the sea.

The lifeboats had pulled away from the *Titanic.* They wanted to avoid being pulled down with her in the suction of the sinking ship. Now the people in the lifeboats assessed the spot they were in. The *Titanic* had been carrying over 2,200 passengers. The lifeboats had a capacity of 1,178. However, in the confusion and in the disbelief that the ship would sink, only 711 people had secured places in the boats.

Twenty minutes after the *Titanic* had slid under the sea, the *Carpathia* arrived on the scene in response to the *Titanic's* SOS. The *Carpathia's* searchlight probed the night expecting to find the great ship. But the beams of light picked up only small boats—some all but empty—bobbing about on the sea. The unsinkable *Titanic* had carried over 1,500 people with her to a watery grave. The *Carpathia* took the 711 survivors aboard. Then the liner headed for New York at her best speed.

Titanic and the passengers and crew members she carried with her lay undisturbed in their watery grave for almost three quarters of a century. Over those long years, many expeditions searched for the remains of the *Titanic.* In 1985, *Alvin,* a midget sub designed for deep water exploration, joined the search. *Alvin* succeeded in finding *Titanic's* rusty remains. The liner lay in two pieces, more than two and one-half miles down. The ship's bow had plunged fifty feet into the muddy bottom before settling down into the sand. The rear half of the ship, badly broken up, lay some distance away. Scattered about the wreckage for some distance were reminders of the passengers she had carried. Video cameras aboard *Alvin* scanned the sea bottom. They picked up images of bottles of champagne, china cups and saucers, and the head of a little girl's doll.

The crew of the midget sub placed a bronze tablet near *Titanic's* stern. The marker is in memory of the 1,522 lost souls who perished with the great ship. May she and they Rest in Peace. ■

Find out your reading time and enter it on the SCORECARD. Then turn to page 156 and look up your reading speed. Write the Words per Minute on the SCORECARD.

Now go on to the exercises in "How Well Did You Read?" Use the SCORECARD to record your critical reading scores. When the SCORECARD is full, transfer your Words per Minute and Critical Reading Score to the graphs on pages 158 and 159.

SCORECARD

Reading Speed

Reading Time _____ : _____
Minutes Seconds

Words per Minute [   ]

How Well Did You Read?

Using Words Precisely ——

Choosing the Best Title ——

Recognizing Important Details ——

Finding the Main Idea ——

Critical Reading Score [   ]
(Add the 4 scores above)

8. Death of the Unsinkable *Titanic*

How Well Did You Read?

Answer the four types of questions that follow. The directions for each type of question tell you how to mark and score your answers.

After you have answered all the questions, check your work using the Answer Key on page 149. If you have the right answer, write the score on the gray line next to the answer. If your answer is wrong, write 0 on the line.

Then add your scores for each type of question and write the total scores in the gray brackets. Enter the four total scores on the SCORECARD and add them to find your Critical Reading Score.

A Using Words Precisely

	Answer	Score
Mark the word or phrase that has the *same* meaning as the underlined word	(S)	3
Mark the word or phrase that has *almost the same* meaning as the underlined word	(A)	1
Mark the word or phrase that is the *opposite* of the underlined word	(O)	1

	Answer	Score
1. Smith wanted to prove that the *Titanic* was the world's most <u>luxurious</u> ship.		
a. poor, lacking in comfort	(O)	——
b. ornate, highly decorated	(S)	——
c. splendid and comfortable	(A)	——
2. Lookout Fred Fleet <u>peered</u> ahead from his position high up on the mast.		
a. looked to see more clearly	(S)	——
b. watched with interest	(A)	——
c. ignored the view	(O)	——

A Using Words Precisely (continued)

Answer   Score

3. The occupants of the boats watched with a grim <u>fascination</u>.

   a. lively interest ____

   b. powerful attraction ____

   c. indifference ____

4. Now the people in the boats <u>assessed</u> the spot they were in.

   a. ignored ____

   b. took stock of ____

   c. estimated ____

5. The passengers in the boats became afraid that the tiny crafts would <u>capsize</u>.

   a. overturn ____

   b. hold upright ____

   c. sway from side to side ____

Using Words Precisely Score [ ]

B Choosing the Best Title

Answer   Score

Mark the *best title* .... (T)   10

Mark the title that is *too broad* .... (B)   5

Mark the title that is *too narrow* .... (N)   5

Answer   Score

1. The Death of the *Titanic* ____

2. The *Titanic* Hits an Iceberg ____

3. First Voyage of the *Titanic* ____

Choosing the Best Title Score [ ]

C — Recognizing Important Details

	Answer	Score
Mark the details that are *true*	(T)	5
Mark the details that are *false*	(F)	5
Mark the details that are *not mentioned* in the article	(N)	5

	Answer	Score
1. The *Titanic* sailed from Southampton, England, to New York on its first voyage.	(T)	___
2. The *Titanic* would not have hit the iceberg if it had had lookouts on duty.	(N)	___
3. The *Titanic*'s lifeboats carried blankets which proved useful in the chill of the North Atlantic.	(N)	___
4. When the *Titanic*'s orchestra began to play hymns, the passengers realized the ship was doomed.	(N)	___
5. The iceberg slashed open many of the *Titanic*'s watertight compartments.	(T)	___
6. The *Titanic*'s pumps could have handled the water coming in if the crew had been able to keep generating electricity.	(N)	___
7. Sleeping passengers came tumbling on deck in panic when the *Titanic* crashed into the iceberg.	(N)	___

Recognizing Important Details Score [ ]

D — Finding the Main Idea

	Answer	Score
Mark the *main idea*	(M)	10
Mark the statement that is *too broad*	(B)	5
Mark the statement that is *too narrow*	(N)	5

	Answer	Score
1. The *Titanic*'s first voyage resulted in a tragic loss of life.	(B)	___
2. The *Titanic* sank with a great loss of life after ripping open its side on an iceberg.	(M)	___
3. The *Titanic* tore a 300-foot gash in its side when it hit an iceberg.	(N)	___

Finding the Main Idea Score [ ]

Galveston, Texas, is located on a narrow strip of land barely high enough to rise above the waters of the Gulf of Mexico. When a 1900 hurricane whipped up the waves, the citizens found themselves actually looking *up* at the water. Then, the waves descended and destroyed the city.

9

Galveston: The City That Drowned

Read this article well enough so that you can answer questions about it. Your teacher may want you to keep track of your reading time. If so, write your reading time on the SCORECARD on page 67 after you finish the article.

Then answer the questions about the article to find out how well you understood what you read. These questions will help you sharpen your reading and thinking skills.

It was the sea that had made Galveston, Texas, a great city at the turn of this century. And it was the sea that made it the scene of the greatest natural disaster in United States history. The island of Galveston, in 1900, was the fastest growing port in the country. Galveston owed its prosperity to its location on the Gulf of Mexico. Dozens of steamship lines maintained piers and offices in the city. The island had become a shore resort. Texas millionaires had built magnificent houses along the beach.

The people of Galveston were so busy making money and building their city that they didn't have time to worry about danger from the sea. Their island city had been built on a sandbar that was only a mile wide at its narrowest point. The average height of the land was only nine feet above sea level.

In September, 1900, the Weather Bureau had been tracking a hurricane for several days. The hurricane had started in the West Indies and was moving northwest toward Texas. A few worried people called the Weather Bureau. The Director of Galveston's Weather Bureau, Dr. Isaac M. Cline, advised callers to leave the island.

The storm was now four days old. Its winds had reached the speed of 125 miles per hour. The Gulf of Mexico began to boil. The surf became unusually high. All electricity was out. The bridges connecting the island with the mainland had gone down before the onslaught of wind and water. The entire city was under water. The people of Galveston were trapped; there was no escape. Many gathered in a tall hotel in the center of town. The water level continued to rise. At one point the sea rose four feet in four seconds. High tide came in twenty feet above normal—in a city only nine feet above sea level.

Weather Bureau chief Cline's own house caved in, and his wife drowned.

Dr. Cline, his youngest child and his brother were swept out to sea. They whirled about in the swirling waters till an incoming tide washed them ashore, still alive, on a Galveston beach.

A journalist from the nearby city of Houston described the disaster for his newspaper. He wrote, "...streets were submerged to a depth of ten feet. To leave a house was to drown. To remain was to court death in the wreckage." The reporter described scenes of death and destruction at schools, orphan asylums, hospitals and old people's homes. Bruised and bleeding women carrying the lifeless bodies of children were an all-too-common sight.

A Catholic orphanage operated by the Sisters of Charity stood directly in the hurricane's path. The sisters, knowing that the orphanage would be washed away, tied the children to them. The moment the waters went down, would-be rescuers arrived at the orphanage. They found that more than 100 of the children and all the nuns had perished. The small bodies of the orphans were found tied together in groups of eight. Each group was tied to a rope passed around a dead nun's waist.

Rescue efforts got underway as soon as the waters started to recede. The work was hampered by an intense spell of hot weather. The heat made the already unbearable suffering even more horrible. There was the danger that the already swollen bodies would breed an epidemic. The corpses of 6,000 people and countless animals had to be disposed of. The saturated ground couldn't be used for graves.

Then catastrophe followed catastrophe, each more macabre than the one before. Looters came out to rob the dead of jewelry and money. When a dead person's finger was too swollen to remove a ring, the looters hacked off the finger. One looter was found with twenty-three severed fingers.

The desperate city authorities had hundreds of corpses hauled out to sea for burial. When the tide shifted, however, the bodies washed back to the city's beaches. Corpses were gathered and ignited in huge funeral pyres.

The sheer horror of the catastrophe caused many of the citizens of Galveston to leave the city. Most residents, however, stayed in Galveston and resolved never to let such a tragedy strike again. There was no way they could prevent hurricane winds. But they could do something about the floods stirred up by those winds. They built a huge stone seawall to protect the city from the waters of the gulf.

The people of Galveston quickly rebuilt their city behind the new seawall. In 1915, almost exactly on the fifteenth anniversary of the great horror, another powerful hurricane struck Galveston. This time, the city's seawall protected it from the full force of the waves. The second hurricane did claim 275 lives. The city, however, was spared most of the horror of 1900. ■

Find out your reading time and enter it on the SCORECARD. Then turn to page 156 and look up your reading speed. Write the Words per Minute on the SCORECARD.

Now go on to the exercises in "How Well Did You Read?" Use the SCORE-CARD to record your critical reading scores. When the SCORECARD is full, transfer your Words per Minute and Critical Reading Score to the graphs on pages 158 and 159.

SCORECARD

Reading Speed

Reading Time _____ : _____

Minutes   Seconds

Words per Minute [   ]

How Well Did You Read?

Using Words Precisely ——

Choosing the Best Title ——

Recognizing Important Details ——

Finding the Main Idea ——

Critical Reading Score [   ]
(Add the 4 scores above)

9. Galveston: The City That Drowned

How Well Did You Read?

Answer the four types of questions that follow. The directions for each type of question tell you how to mark and score your answers.

After you have answered all the questions, check your work using the Answer Key on page 149. If you have the right answer, write the score on the gray line next to the answer. If your answer is wrong, write 0 on the line.

Then add your scores for each type of question and write the total scores in the gray brackets. Enter the four total scores on the SCORECARD and add them to find your Critical Reading Score.

A — Using Words Precisely

	Answer	Score
Mark the word or phrase that has the *same* meaning as the underlined word	(S)	3
Mark the word or phrase that has *almost the same* meaning as the underlined word	(A)	1
Mark the word or phrase that is the *opposite* of the underlined word	(O)	1

	Answer	Score
1. The bridges had gone down before the <u>onslaught</u> of wind and water.		
a. attack	( )	——
b. push	( )	——
c. retreat	( )	——
2. Rescue efforts got under way as soon as the waters started to <u>recede.</u>		
a. move forward	( )	——
b. move back	( )	——
c. move away	( )	——

A — Using Words Precisely (continued)

Answer   Score

3. Their work was <u>hampered</u> by an intense spell of hot weather.

    a. held back   ( ) ___

    b. assisted   ( ) ___

    c. halted   ( ) ___

4. The <u>saturated</u> ground couldn't be used for graves.

    a. wet   ( ) ___

    b. soaked   ( ) ___

    c. dry   ( ) ___

5. Then catastrophe followed catastrophe, each more <u>macabre</u> than the one before.

    a. grim   ( ) ___

    b. pleasant   ( ) ___

    c. gruesome   ( ) ___

Using Words Precisely Score [ ]

B — Choosing the Best Title

Answer   Score

Mark the *best title* .... (**T**) <u>10</u>

Mark the title that is *too broad* .... (**B**) <u>5</u>

Mark the title that is *too narrow* .... (**N**) <u>5</u>

Answer   Score

1. Hurricane Winds of 125 Miles per Hour Destroyed Galveston ( ) ___

2. Flood and Hurricane Destroy Galveston ( ) ___

3. The Destruction of Galveston ( ) ___

Choosing the Best Title Score [ ]

C — Recognizing Important Details

	Answer	Score
Mark the details that are *true*	(T)	5
Mark the details that are *false*	(F)	5
Mark the details that are *not mentioned* in the article	(N)	5

	Answer	Score
1. Galveston was a rich city at the turn of the century.	( )	___
2. Galveston Island was only a mile wide at its narrowest point.	( )	___
3. Weather Bureau Chief Cline lost his life in the hurricane and flood.	( )	___
4. Many families kept the bodies of drowned relatives on the roofs of tall houses that were above water.	( )	___
5. The horror would have been greater if the weather had not remained cool.	( )	___
6. The police, in rowboats, directed boat traffic on the flooded streets.	( )	___
7. The nuns were able to save the lives of a group of orphans by tying the children to them.	( )	___

Recognizing Important Details Score [ ]

D — Finding the Main Idea

	Answer	Score
Mark the *main idea*	(M)	10
Mark the statement that is *too broad*	(B)	5
Mark the statement that is *too narrow*	(N)	5

	Answer	Score
1. Thousands of people perished in the greatest natural catastrophe in United States history.	( )	___
2. Flood tides more than twenty feet above normal swept over Galveston, Texas, killing thousands.	( )	___
3. Galveston's location contributed to its destruction by hurricane and flood.	( )	___

Finding the Main Idea Score [ ]

The Cocoanut Grove, Boston's biggest, fanciest, most glamorous nightclub, was really swinging when fire broke out. In seconds, laughter changed to screams. People who had been dancing suddenly found themselves fleeing for their lives. This photograph taken after the fire shows how complete the destruction was.

10

Boston's Cocoanut Grove Ablaze

Read this article well enough so that you can answer questions about it. Your teacher may want you to keep track of your reading time. If so, write your reading time on the SCORECARD on page 73 after you finish the article.

Then answer the questions about the article to find out how well you understood what you read. These questions will help you sharpen your reading and thinking skills.

There was a tremendous crowd at Boston's Cocoanut Grove nightclub. On November 28, 1942, the club held twice its legal capacity of 500 people. The United States was involved in World War II, and the Cocoanut Grove was crowded with soldiers ready to sail for Europe, and with sailors from Boston's big naval base. Other patrons were celebrating that afternoon's football game between Holy Cross and Boston College. Warplant workers, their pockets bulging with overtime pay, rounded out the crowd.

The Cocoanut Grove, as its name suggests, was fitted out to look like a South Seas paradise with bamboo and palm trees swaying under blue tropical skies. The South Seas glamour was, unfortunately, all flammable paper and cloth. The blue skies were blue satin cloth, the bamboo was made of paper, and the palm trees placed near every table and chair were also paper.

On that fateful night, one of the guests wanted the room known as the Melody Lounge to be even darker, and unscrewed a lightbulb from the ceiling. Stanley Tomaszewski was a sixteen-year-old busboy at the Cocoanut Grove. His job was to clear tables of dirty glasses and plates. When a bartender saw how dark the Melody Lounge was, he ordered the busboy to replace the missing bulb. Tomaszewski climbed up onto a chair with a bulb, but couldn't see where to screw in the new light. He lit a match and held it up until he burned his fingers. In pain, Tomaszewski dropped the match. A paper palm tree caught fire and ignited the blue cloth sky. The fire jumped quickly from the ceiling to the paper palms and bamboo. A bartender swiped at the fire with a wet towel, and then used a fire extinguisher. For a brief time the fire was confined to the Melody Lounge, the room where it started. The sparks, however, quickly spread.

Guests in the nightclub's two other lounges were unaware of any danger. Band leader Mickey Alpert was about to open the evening's entertainment with "The Star-Spangled Banner." Suddenly, there was a cry of, "Fire!" and a woman, her dress and hair ablaze, ran into the bar. In seconds, she had set a tablecloth on fire and the flames were jumping from paper palm to paper palm. The flames spread so rapidly that people who were eating or dancing one moment, were the next moment trying to beat fire from their hair and clothing.

There was a mad rush for the doors. Some army and naval officers tried to calm the crowd, but the rush went on picking up a panicky momentum. Most of the crowd knew only one way out: the main entrance through which they had come in. It had a revolving door, and the crowd's pushing and shoving knocked the door off its axis so that it couldn't be turned either way. Later, when police and fire fighters tried to enter the club, they found the door blocked by hundreds of bodies piled high. The club had a total of a dozen doors. The other doors, however, opened inward and couldn't be opened as people pushed against the doors. As the doorways became blocked with bodies, people milled about, confused, in the smoke and darkness.

Vocalist Bill Payne of the Alpert Band led twenty people out of the club by passing under the stage, through a refrigerator room in the basement, and out to the safety of the street.

Other people managed to escape by running upstairs to the Cocoanut Grove's roof. They then jumped onto the tops of autos parked in the streets below.

Every available vehicle was used to rush seriously wounded people to hospitals. In addition to ambulances, cars, express trucks, newspaper delivery trucks, taxis and even a moving van were pressed into service.

The injured benefited from new methods and drugs perfected in the early days of the war. The use of blood plasma saved many lives. So, too, did the use of the new wonder drugs, sulfa and penicillin.

When Boston doctors ran out of sulfa drugs, they put in a call to New York City. A supply of the wonder drugs was assembled and flown up to Boston, arriving there only one hour and twelve minutes after the call went out.

Inside the Cocoanut Grove, the fire spread so rapidly that 491 people died, mostly from smoke inhalation. In addition, over 200 other people were scarred or crippled as a result of the fire.

Boston's fire and police departments and Civil Defense workers were quick to respond to the emergency. A group of naval officers and sailors linked arms and formed a human chain to hold back the crowd of thousands that gathered. Members of the Army, Navy and Coast Guard helped fire fighters with their hose lines. They had the fire out in one hour even though they had to force their way into the jam of bodies behind the nightclub's doors.

After the fire was out, people began to assign blame for it. The Boston newspapers blamed busboy Stanley Tomaszewski. The public disagreed. Hundreds of people wrote letters to the sixteen-year-old boy assuring him that the fire had not been his fault. And the Boston Fire Department, which investigated the fire, stated that it was unable to find that Tomaszewski's conduct had started the fire.

The real villain was the panic and the blind, unreasoning rush to the exits. Experts believe that if people had remained calm, there would have been few, if any, deaths. ■

Find out your reading time and enter it on the SCORECARD. Then turn to page 156 and look up your reading speed. Write the Words per Minute on the SCORECARD.

Now go on to the exercises in "How Well Did You Read?" Use the SCORECARD to record your critical reading scores. When the SCORECARD is full, transfer your Words per Minute and Critical Reading Score to the graphs on pages 158 and 159.

SCORECARD

Reading Speed

Reading Time _____ : _____
                 Minutes   Seconds

Words per Minute [   ]

How Well Did You Read?

Using Words Precisely _____

Choosing the Best Title _____

Recognizing Important Details _____

Finding the Main Idea _____

Critical Reading Score [   ]
(Add the 4 scores above)

10. Boston's Cocoanut Grove Ablaze

How Well Did You Read?

Answer the four types of questions that follow. The directions for each type of question tell you how to mark and score your answers.

After you have answered all the questions, check your work using the Answer Key on page 150. If you have the right answer, write the score on the gray line next to the answer. If your answer is wrong, write 0 on the line.

Then add your scores for each type of question and write the total scores in the gray brackets. Enter the four total scores on the SCORECARD and add them to find your Critical Reading Score.

A — Using Words Precisely

	Answer	Score
Mark the word or phrase that has the *same* meaning as the underlined word	(S)	3
Mark the word or phrase that has *almost the same* meaning as the underlined word	(A)	1
Mark the word or phrase that is the *opposite* of the underlined word	(O)	1

	Answer	Score
1. The rush went on, picking up a panicky <u>momentum</u>.		
a. constant speed	( )	___
b. gain in speed	( )	___
c. loss of speed	( )	___
2. People <u>milled</u> <u>about</u>, confused, in the smoke and darkness.		
a. moved purposefully	( )	___
b. moved slowly	( )	___
c. moved aimlessly	( )	___

A — Using Words Precisely (continued)

Answer   Score

3. For a brief time, the fire was <u>confined</u> to the room where it started.

   a. spread out   ( ) ___

   b. kept in   ( ) ___

   c. kept near   ( ) ___

4. Ambulances, cars, trucks and taxis were <u>pressed</u> <u>into</u> <u>service</u>.

   a. selected in a crisis   ( ) ___

   b. made to serve in a crisis   ( ) ___

   c. not used because of a crisis   ( ) ___

5. The injured benefited from new drugs <u>perfected</u> in the early days of the world war.

   a. reached final development   ( ) ___

   b. forgotten about   ( ) ___

   c. improved significantly   ( ) ___

Using Words Precisely Score   [ ]

B — Choosing the Best Title

Answer   Score

Mark the *best title* . . . . (**T**)   <u>10</u>

Mark the title that is *too broad* . . . . (**B**)   <u>5</u>

Mark the title that is *too narrow* . . . . (**N**)   <u>5</u>

Answer   Score

1. A Terrible Fire in Boston   ( ) ___

2. Hundreds Die in Boston Nightclub Fire   ( ) ___

3. Match Sets Fire to Paper Palm Trees   ( ) ___

Choosing the Best Title Score

C — Recognizing Important Details

	Answer	Score
Mark the details that are *true*	(T)	5
Mark the details that are *false*	(F)	5
Mark the details that are *not mentioned* in the article	(N)	5

	Answer	Score
1. The Cocoanut Grove held more than the legal number of people.	( )	___
2. The blue skies of the Cocoanut Grove were made of blue cloth.	( )	___
3. Busboy Stanley Tomaszewski was working to save money for college.	( )	___
4. Army and naval officers led many people to safety by passing under the stage and through the basement.	( )	___
5. Boston obtained drugs from New York City in just twelve hours and one minute.	( )	___
6. Some newspapers blamed busboy Tomaszewski for having started the fire.	( )	___
7. The Cocoanut Grove was rebuilt bigger and better in less than a year after the fire.	( )	___

Recognizing Important Details Score [ ]

D — Finding the Main Idea

	Answer	Score
Mark the *main idea*	(M)	10
Mark the statement that is *too broad*	(B)	5
Mark the statement that is *too narrow*	(N)	5

	Answer	Score
1. Hundreds of people lost their lives when a nightclub caught fire.	( )	___
2. Fire fighters, police officers and members of the armed forces helped the survivors of the Cocoanut Grove fire.	( )	___
3. Hundreds of people died in the panic that followed when the Cocoanut Grove caught fire.	( )	___

Finding the Main Idea Score [ ]

A hundred years ago, Krakatoa, an island in the South Pacific, all but vanished in a volcanic eruption. All over the world—thousands of miles from Krakatoa—people heard the noise of its death. Scientists say the eruption was the loudest noise ever heard on this planet. In this photo taken in 1960, Anak Krakatoa—"Child of Krakatoa," a small island that emerged close to the remnants of the original volcano—looks threatening, but not nearly so threatening as its "parent" did one day 77 years earlier.

11

Krakatoa: The Doomsday Crack Heard 'Round the World

Read this article well enough so that you can answer questions about it. Your teacher may want you to keep track of your reading time. If so, write your reading time on the SCORECARD on page 79 after you finish the article.

Then answer the questions about the article to find out how well you understood what you read. These questions will help you sharpen your reading and thinking skills.

In August, 1883, the people of Texas heard a tremendous boom which they thought was cannon fire. What the Texans actually heard was the sound of a series of volcanic eruptions on Krakatoa, an island halfway around the world in the South Pacific. The sound from Krakatoa (now part of Indonesia) was the loudest noise in human history.

Krakatoa was a small island—only six miles square—between Java and Sumatra. It almost disappeared from the face of the earth, and the noise of its passing was heard halfway around the world. On Borneo, 350 miles from Krakatoa, the islanders believed the sound was caused by an evil spirit seeking revenge. They managed to escape from the spirit, but only by jumping off a cliff and killing themselves.

Noise was not the volcano's only way of announcing its eruption. A cloud of steam and ash rose to a height of more than 36,000 feet—more than seven miles. A ship more than fifteen miles from Krakatoa was covered with volcanic ash fifteen feet deep. Ash fell on ships as far as 1,600 miles from Krakatoa, and eventually covered an area of 300,000 square miles.

Some of the lava that also spewed from the volcano mixed with air and hardened into a stone called *pumice*. The air in pumice makes it so light that it floats. Pumice from Krakatoa was blown into the sea where ocean currents spread it over a large area of the Pacific. For eighteen months after the eruption, ships plowed through seas covered with great chunks of floating pumice. Then the pumice stones absorbed so much water that they lost their buoyancy and sank.

The volcano's light volcanic ash and dust rose into the atmosphere where winds carried it all over the earth. Weather all over the globe was affected for months after the eruption. For an entire year, the umbrella of dust permitted only 87 percent of the usual amount of sunlight to reach the earth. For two years, the reflection of the sun on the ash in the upper atmosphere resulted in spectacular sunsets. Sunsets were blue in South America; green in Panama. The skies over the United States glowed so red that people thought their color was the result of gigantic fires. People turned in fire alarms in Poughkeepsie, New York and in New Haven, Connecticut.

The great shock wave generated by the eruption swept completely around the world and kept right on going. It circled the globe once—twice—seven times in all.

Krakatoa's eruption was accompanied by a great earthquake. The quake included the seabed under the waters surrounding the island. The seas around Krakatoa rose to a temperature sixty degrees Fahrenheit above normal. A great *tsunami* (sü-nä'-mē), a wave originating under water, rolled out from the island. The tsunami reached a height of 135 feet and attained a speed of 600 miles per hour.

It was this great hill of moving water that caused most of the 36,000 casualties associated with Krakatoa. The wave spread out in all directions and wiped out more than 300 villages in Southeast Asia. The tsunami picked up a gunboat and dropped it at a point thirty feet above sea level and more than a mile inland. All of the gunboat's crew members were killed.

Giant tidal waves raced from Krakatoa to all parts of the globe. Their effects were felt as far away as the English Channel, 13,073 miles away.

Krakatoa itself was torn to pieces. Five cubic miles of rock—as much as in some of the world's tallest mountains—was blown into dust. Three-fourths of the island disappeared into dust and air. Those parts of the island that didn't explode into the air sank into the sea. Parts of the island that had been a thousand feet above sea level now lay a thousand feet under the ocean.

After the eruption, the small piece of Krakatoa that was left was covered with volcanic dust. There was no grass, no shrubs, no trees. A single red spider—the only living thing that survived the eruption—spun its web, a web for which there were no more insects.

In 1925, a small peak popped up out of the sea next to Krakatoa. More and more of the peak emerged from the sea until a new island was formed. The South Pacific islanders named the newcomer *Anak Krakatoa,* Child of Krakatoa. In 1928,

three years after its birth, Anak Krakatoa had a minor eruption. The island continues to emerge from the sea to grow larger and larger.

What will be the fate of Anak Krakatoa? Will it grow into a full-sized island? Will it have a gigantic volcanic eruption? Only time will tell. ■

Find out your reading time and enter it on the SCORECARD. Then turn to page 156 and look up your reading speed. Write the Words per Minute on the SCORECARD.

Now go on to the exercises in "How Well Did You Read?" Use the SCORECARD to record your critical reading scores. When the SCORECARD is full, transfer your Words per Minute and Critical Reading Score to the graphs on pages 158 and 159.

SCORECARD

Reading Speed

Reading Time _____ : _____
Minutes   Seconds

Words per Minute [   ]

How Well Did You Read?

Using Words Precisely _____

Choosing the Best Title _____

Recognizing Important Details _____

Finding the Main Idea _____

Critical Reading Score [   ]
(Add the 4 scores above)

**11. Krakatoa: The Doomsday Crack
Heard 'Round the World**

How Well Did You Read?

Answer the four types of questions that follow. The directions for each type of question tell you how to mark and score your answers.

After you have answered all the questions, check your work using the Answer Key on page 150. If you have the right answer, write the score on the gray line next to the answer. If your answer is wrong, write 0 on the line.

Then add your scores for each type of question and write the total scores in the gray brackets. Enter the four total scores on the SCORECARD and add them to find your Critical Reading Score.

A   Using Words Precisely

	Answer	Score
Mark the word or phrase that has the *same* meaning as the underlined word	(S)	3
Mark the word or phrase that has *almost the same* meaning as the underlined word	(A)	1
Mark the word or phrase that is the *opposite* of the underlined word	(O)	1

	Answer	Score
1. The pumice stones absorbed so much water that they lost their <u>buoyancy</u> and sank.		
a. ability to float	( )	___
b. lightness in weight	( )	___
c. ability to submerge	( )	___
2. The lava that <u>spewed</u> from the volcano mixed with air and became pumice.		
a. fell into	( )	___
b. burst out of	( )	___
c. came out of	( )	___

A Using Words Precisely (continued)

Answer Score

3. The great shock wave <u>generated</u> by the eruption swept completely around the world.

   a. influenced by ( ) ___

   b. happening independently ( ) ___

   c. caused by ( ) ___

4. The tsunami rose to a height of 135 feet and <u>attained</u> a speed of 600 miles per hour.

   a. missed ( ) ___

   b. had ( ) ___

   c. reached ( ) ___

5. The island continues to <u>emerge</u> from the sea and to grow larger and larger.

   a. be seen ( ) ___

   b. come forth ( ) ___

   c. go back ( ) ___

Using Words Precisely Score [ ]

B Choosing the Best Title

Answer Score

Mark the *best title* .... (T) <u>10</u>

Mark the title that is *too broad* .... (B) <u>5</u>

Mark the title that is *too narrow* .... (N) <u>5</u>

Answer Score

1. Krakatoa Makes World's Loudest Noise ( ) ___

2. A Great Volcano Erupts ( ) ___

3. The Eruption That Destroyed Krakatoa ( ) ___

Choosing the Best Title Score [ ]

C — Recognizing Important Details

	Answer	Score
Mark the details that are *true*	(T)	5
Mark the details that are *false*	(F)	5
Mark the details that are *not mentioned* in the article	(N)	5

	Answer	Score
1. The sound of the eruptions on Krakatoa could be heard in Chicago.	( )	___
2. Volcanic ash from Krakatoa covered 300,000 square miles.	( )	___
3. Pumice from Krakatoa floated for eighteen years.	( )	___
4. Red, green and blue sunsets followed Krakatoa's eruption.	( )	___
5. Krakatoa's shock wave circled the earth seven times.	( )	___
6. Most of the people in the villages by the tsunami were warned in time to escape.	( )	___
7. Anak Krakatoa has already grown bigger than Krakatoa itself.	( )	___

Recognizing Important Details Score [ ]

D — Finding the Main Idea

	Answer	Score
Mark the *main idea*	(M)	10
Mark the statement that is *too broad*	(B)	5
Mark the statement that is *too narrow*	(N)	5

	Answer	Score
1. Krakatoa disappeared in a gigantic eruption whose effects were felt worldwide.	( )	___
2. Krakatoa is a dramatic example of the power of volcanoes.	( )	___
3. Krakatoa's eruption and tsunami resulted in 36,000 deaths.	( )	___

Finding the Main Idea Score [ ]

It was 1917. World War I raged in Europe. The city of Halifax, Nova Scotia, was sending munitions to the Allies. Halifax harbor was armed against German submarines and German airships. One danger Halifax was not prepared for was a harbor accident that would ignite the tons of explosives. But that's exactly what happened. And in less than one minute, 16,000 people were dead and 3,000 acres were destroyed.

12

Halifax: City Blown to Pieces

Read this article well enough so that you can answer questions about it. Your teacher may want you to keep track of your reading time. If so, write your reading time on the SCORECARD on page 85 after you finish the article.

Then answer the questions about the article to find out how well you understood what you read. These questions will help you sharpen your reading and thinking skills.

The United States and Canada shipped vast quantities of war material to the Allies during World War I. Millions of tons of munitions passed through the Canadian port of Halifax, Nova Scotia. Because the citizens of the city feared an attack by German *zeppelins* (dirigibles or airships), artillery batteries had been set along the shore. To prevent underwater attacks, anti-submarine nets had been strung at the entrance to the harbor. That harbor was reached by way of a long channel only a mile wide. The channel was appropriately named "the narrows."

On the morning of December 6, 1917, a French ship, the *Mont Blanc*, was threading its way through the channel. It was bound for Europe with a load of munitions. The *Mont Blanc* was a floating bomb. Its cargo consisted of 7,000 tons of TNT and other explosives, plus 9,000 gallons of benzene, a highly flammable liquid.

Heading toward the *Mont Blanc* in "the narrows" was a freighter, the *Imo*, returning empty from Belgium. The *Imo* blew its whistle to signal that it would pass the *Mont Blanc* to starboard. For some reason never explained, the *Imo* continued on straight toward the *Mont Blanc*. The captain of the *Mont Blanc* realized that he couldn't get his ship out of the *Imo*'s path. He did, however, manage to maneuver the vessel so that the approaching ship would not strike its cargo of TNT. The *Imo*'s bow sliced the *Mont Blanc* all the way down to the waterline. It also sliced open the *Mont Blanc*'s cargo of benzene. The highly flammable liquid spilled down in the ship's hold, where it caught fire. The blazing fuel flowed toward the 7,000 tons of explosives.

The *Mont Blanc*'s crew knew that their lives depended on putting out the flames. Although the French sailors fought desperately, the rapidly spreading flames drove them back, foot-by-foot. The captain realized that the struggle was hopeless and gave the order to abandon ship. The crew needed no urging. They knew that it was a life or death matter to get clear of the ship before it blew up. They rowed for their lives. When their boat reached the shore they jumped out and kept right on fleeing.

The *Mont Blanc* and its explosive cargo drifted toward the piers of Halifax. A British warship, the *High Flyer*, had been waiting to convoy the *Mont Blanc* to Europe and protect it from attack by German subs. Now the crew aboard the *High Flyer* realized that it was the city of Halifax that needed protecting—and from the *Mont Blanc*. A boatload of British sailors set out for the blazing vessel, intending to sink it before it could explode. They reached the burning ship and had just climbed to its deck when the *Mont Blanc* blew up with a boom heard six miles away. It simply disappeared. Many citizens of Halifax were sure that the long-expected zeppelin bombing was underway. Other residents believed that the German Navy had crossed the Atlantic and was shelling them.

At least two-thirds of the sailors on the

ships in Halifax harbor died instantly. The *Mont Blanc*'s blast set off other explosions among the stacks of munitions on the piers. About 3,000 acres—including homes, factories and schools—were destroyed by the explosions and the fires that followed them. Only 10 pupils out of 500 survived the blast. It is thought that a total of 16,000 people lost their lives and 8,000 were badly injured. The exact death toll will never be known, however, since some entire families were wiped out.

A telegrapher named Vincent Coleman played one of the most heroic roles that day in a city of heroes. Coleman saw a ship on fire and realized that it was the munitions ship scheduled to dock that morning. He telegraphed: "A munitions ship is on fire and headed for Pier Eight. Goodbye." It was truly goodbye for Coleman; he died in the explosion. His message, however, started help on the way within fifteen minutes of the blast. People from all over Canada and from the northeastern United States sent food, blankets, cots, medical supplies, lumber and window glass. The survivors soon had most of the things they needed.

One survivor of the disaster was the steamship, the *Imo*, the ship that had rammed the *Mont Blanc*. When the *Mont Blanc* exploded, the *Imo* was blown clear out of the water onto the shore. The ship was rebuilt and refloated under a new name. Four years after the Halifax explosion, the *Imo* struck a reef in the South Atlantic and sank.

The city of Halifax itself emerged much better from the disaster. There was little of the rioting and looting so common in other calamities. Druggists gave away free medical supplies and restaurants provided free meals. Halifax was soon nicknamed "The City of Comrades." Working together as comrades, the survivors of Halifax soon rebuilt their town. Today's Halifax is a strong and modern city. ■

Find out your reading time and enter it on the SCORECARD. Then turn to page 157 and look up your reading speed. Write the Words per Minute on the SCORECARD.

Now go on to the exercises in "How Well Did You Read?" Use the SCORECARD to record your critical reading scores. When the SCORECARD is full, transfer your Words per Minute and Critical Reading Score to the graphs on pages 158 and 159.

SCORECARD

Reading Speed

Reading Time _____ : _____
Minutes   Seconds

Words per Minute [   ]

How Well Did You Read?

Using Words Precisely ——

Choosing the Best Title ——

Recognizing Important Details ——

Finding the Main Idea ——

Critical Reading Score [   ]
(Add the 4 scores above)

12. Halifax: City Blown to Pieces

How Well Did You Read?

Answer the four types of questions that follow. The directions for each type of question tell you how to mark and score your answers.

After you have answered all the questions, check your work using the Answer Key on page 150. If you have the right answer, write the score on the gray line next to the answer. If your answer is wrong, write 0 on the line.

Then add your scores for each type of question and write the total scores in the gray brackets. Enter the four total scores on the SCORECARD and add them to find your Critical Reading Score.

A Using Words Precisely

	Answer	Score
Mark the word or phrase that has the *same* meaning as the underlined word	(S)	3
Mark the word or phrase that has *almost the same* meaning as the underlined word	(A)	1
Mark the word or phrase that is the *opposite* of the underlined word	(O)	1

	Answer	Score

1. A French ship, the *Mont Blanc*, was <u>threading</u> its way through the channel.

   a. passing slowly through a narrow place ( ) ____

   b. moving quickly through a broad passage ( ) ____

   c. moving slowly and carefully ( ) ____

2. The captain managed to <u>maneuver</u> the vessel so its cargo of TNT was not struck.

   a. turn backward ( ) ____

   b. change position ( ) ____

   c. maintain a course ( ) ____

A — Using Words Precisely (continued)

Answer   Score

3. When their boat reached the shore, the sailors jumped out and kept right on <u>fleeing</u>.

    a. facing a danger   ( ) ___

    b. leaving quickly   ( ) ___

    c. running from danger   ( ) ___

4. The *High Flyer* had been waiting to <u>convoy</u> the *Mont Blanc* to Europe.

    a. escort and guard   ( ) ___

    b. accompany on a trip   ( ) ___

    c. leave on a solitary voyage   ( ) ___

5. The exact death <u>toll</u> will never be known since some entire families were wiped out.

    a. number involved   ( ) ___

    b. number who escaped   ( ) ___

    c. number lost   ( ) ___

Using Words Precisely Score   [ ]

B — Choosing the Best Title

Answer   Score

Mark the *best title* .... (T)   <u>10</u>

Mark the title that is *too broad* .... (B)   <u>5</u>

Mark the title that is *too narrow* .... (N)   <u>5</u>

Answer   Score

1. Seven Million Tons of TNT   ( ) ___

2. Halifax, Nova Scotia   ( ) ___

3. The Halifax Explosion   ( ) ___

Choosing the Best Title Score

C — Recognizing Important Details

	Answer	Score
Mark the details that are *true*	(T)	5
Mark the details that are *false*	(F)	5
Mark the details that are *not mentioned* in the article	(N)	5

	Answer	Score
1. The people of Halifax feared a German attack.	( )	___
2. The captain of the *Imo* survived the collision and the explosion.	( )	___
3. The *Mont Blanc*'s crew panicked and disobeyed their captain.	( )	___
4. The British warship, the *High Flyer* had just returned from Europe.	( )	___
5. Sailors from the *High Flyer* hoped to tow the *Mont Blanc* out of the harbor.	( )	___
6. Only 10 pupils out of 500 survived the explosion.	( )	___
7. When telegrapher Vincent Coleman knew he was doomed, he tapped out "goodbye."	( )	___

Recognizing Important Details Score [ ]

D — Finding the Main Idea

	Answer	Score
Mark the *main idea*	(M)	10
Mark the statement that is *too broad*	(B)	5
Mark the statement that is *too narrow*	(N)	5

	Answer	Score
1. A large port in Nova Scotia was destroyed in a wartime accident.	( )	___
2. A munitions ship blew up during World War I and severely damaged Halifax.	( )	___
3. A ship carrying TNT and benzene exploded and killed a total of 16,000 people in 1917.	( )	___

Finding the Main Idea Score [ ]

The Empire State Building juts into the sky above New York City. Three of the busiest airports in the world form a triangle around the great skyscraper. People who gaze in awe at the Empire State often wonder if an airplane has ever collided with the great building. In July, 1945, an Army bomber crashed into the 79th floor, cutting a huge hole in the side of the building, snapping the elevator cables and setting a fire.

Terror in the Fog

On a clear day, a visitor atop the Empire State Building can see for eighty miles. The day was anything but clear that fateful morning in July, 1945.

World War II was still on as Lieutenant Colonel William T. Smith, Jr. piloted his B-25 Bomber toward Newark, New Jersey. Colonel Smith had taken off from Bedford, Massachusetts. He had planned to land at La Guardia Airport in New York City. The La Guardia Airport tower operator had not permitted Smith to land there because of heavy fog. The tower had suggested, instead, a landing at nearby Newark, New Jersey. The tower operator had described the heavy fog over the city by saying, "I can't even see the top of the Empire State Building." So, Colonel Smith headed his bomber toward the alternate landing site. Smith was no newcomer to flying. A twenty-seven-year-old West Point graduate, Smith had logged more than a thousand hours in the air. He had two years of wartime flying in Europe where he had earned three medals as a combat pilot.

Two other people were in the bomber with Smith: another crew member and a sailor hitching a ride home. Albert Penna was going home to comfort his mother who lived in Brooklyn. She had recently lost her only other son in a naval battle in the Pacific. Only a week before, Albert had also flown home to comfort her. Anxious to preserve the life of her remaining son, Penna's mother had made him promise that he wouldn't travel by military aircraft. Despite his promise, he was aboard the bomber as it droned south over New York's Thirty-fourth Street at 225 miles per hour.

Then, as if its pilot suddenly became aware of the building looming before him, the plane swept into a curve. Too late. The bomber crashed with terrifying impact into the wall of the 102-story building. It struck the 79th floor. The explosion was heard two miles away, and a great ball of orange flame billowed out.

For a second, brilliant flames illuminated the skyscraper. Then, the spectators lost sight of the building as it disappeared again in the fog and the smoke from the crash.

When the airplane struck, the impact tore loose both its engines. One motor smashed through seven walls and came out outside the building. It flew through the air and crashed its way through a penthouse atop a smaller building across the street.

The second engine, in flames, cut its way into an elevator shaft and sheared through the cables of a car. A woman passenger was riding in the elevator. Automatic brakes checked the car before it crashed in the basement. But the passenger was trapped in total darkness in the wreckage of the car. Its top had been caved in by the weight of the motor resting on top of it.

Thousands of people in the street below had witnessed the crash. Many of them had been sprinkled with pieces of debris from the crash. Now, most of them stood helpless. One of the witnesses who was anything but helpless was Donald

Maloney. Maloney was a seventeen-year-old Coast Guard hospital apprentice. He ran into a nearby drugstore and ordered the clerk to furnish him with pain killers and other medical supplies. Maloney and other rescuers cut through the side of the wrecked elevator in which the woman was trapped. He then lowered himself into the battered car. When the badly injured passenger looked up she found Maloney administering first aid. "Thank God," she said, "the Navy is here."

A piece of the wrecked plane cut its way into a second of the building's many elevator shafts. The chunk of wreckage cut through the cables supporting a second elevator. The operator, twenty-year-old Betty Lou Oliver, had notified the management that she was leaving her job in a few days. Now, Oliver tried desperately to halt the falling car. Tongues of flame from the blazing gasoline flicked out at her. There was no response to her desperate effort to work the elevator's controls. She had to hang on to the falling car to keep from floating in mid-air. Despite her attempts to stop it, the car plunged to the bottom of the shaft. The floor of the car was pierced when a buffer at the bottom of the shaft crashed through. But the buffer did stop the car. Oliver was bruised and burned, but she was alive after a fall of almost eighty stories.

Many other people were alive only because the crash had occurred on a Saturday. During a weekday, 50,000 people would have been inside the building. Only 1,500 people were at work that Saturday morning. Tragically, many of those at work were in an office at the exact spot where the airplane crashed into the building. The office belonged to the War Relief Services of the National Catholic Welfare Conference. Fire fighters who entered the welfare office found nine badly burned bodies gathered around a single desk. The body of a tenth worker was found at another point in the office. Six stories below, where it had been flung by the crash, the police found another body from the office. Altogether, only fourteen people had been killed in what might easily have been a much greater tragedy.

The disaster might have been avoided altogether if there had been a beacon atop the Empire State Building. Only a day before the crash there had been a discussion about a plan to place such a beacon atop the 102-story skyscraper. Today, a huge light illuminates the skies above the building. In addition, the scores of airplanes coming into La Guardia Airport each day can see the entire top of the skyscraper lit in many colors. ■

Find out your reading time and enter it on the SCORECARD. Then turn to page 157 and look up your reading speed. Write the Words per Minute on the SCORECARD.

Now go on to the exercises in "How Well Did You Read?" Use the SCORECARD to record your critical reading scores. When the SCORECARD is full, transfer your Words per Minute and Critical Reading Score to the graphs on pages 158 and 159.

SCORECARD

Reading Speed

Reading Time _____ : _____
Minutes Seconds

Words per Minute [   ]

How Well Did You Read?

Using Words Precisely _____

Choosing the Best Title _____

Recognizing Important Details _____

Finding the Main Idea _____

Critical Reading Score [   ]
(Add the 4 scores above)

13. Terror in the Fog

How Well Did You Read?

Answer the four types of questions that follow. The directions for each type of question tell you how to mark and score your answers.

After you have answered all the questions, check your work using the Answer Key on page 151. If you have the right answer, write the score on the gray line next to the answer. If your answer is wrong, write 0 on the line.

Then add your scores for each type of question and write the total scores in the gray brackets. Enter the four total scores on the SCORECARD and add them to find your Critical Reading Score.

A Using Words Precisely

	Answer	Score
Mark the word or phrase that has the *same* meaning as the underlined word	(S)	3
Mark the word or phrase that has *almost the same* meaning as the underlined word	(A)	1
Mark the word or phrase that is the *opposite* of the underlined word	(O)	1

Answer   Score

1. The day was anything but clear that <u>fateful</u> morning in July, 1945.

   a. fortunate ( ) _____

   b. unlucky ( ) _____

   c. disastrous ( ) _____

2. Then the pilot suddenly became aware of the building <u>looming</u> before him.

   a. appearing threateningly ( ) _____

   b. appearing in sight ( ) _____

   c. lost to view ( ) _____

A | Using Words Precisely (continued)

Answer   Score

3. When the airplane struck, the <u>impact</u> tore loose both its engines.

   a. contact   ( ) ___

   b. collision   ( ) ___

   c. miss   ( ) ___

4. Automatic brakes <u>checked</u> the car before it crashed in the basement.

   a. stopped   ( ) ___

   b. released   ( ) ___

   c. restrained   ( ) ___

5. <u>Tragically</u>, many were at the exact spot where the airplane crashed into the building.

   a. dreadfully   ( ) ___

   b. happily   ( ) ___

   c. mournfully   ( ) ___

Using Words Precisely Score [ ]

B | Choosing the Best Title

Answer   Score

Mark the *best title* .... (T) 10

Mark the title that is *too broad* .... (B) 5

Mark the title that is *too narrow* .... (N) 5

Answer   Score

1. Tragedy at World's Tallest Building   ( ) ___

2. Elevator Operator Falls 80 Stories   ( ) ___

3. Bomber Crashes Into Empire State Building   ( ) ___

Choosing the Best Title Score

C — Recognizing Important Details

	Answer	Score
Mark the details that are *true*	(**T**)	5
Mark the details that are *false*	(**F**)	5
Mark the details that are *not mentioned* in the article	(**N**)	5

	Answer	Score
1. Colonel Smith was flying to a new assignment.	( )	___
2. Albert Penna was part of the bomber's regular crew.	( )	___
3. Albert Penna's brother had died in an air crash.	( )	___
4. Both engines came off when the bomber crashed.	( )	___
5. Hero Donald Maloney had training as a Coast Guard medic.	( )	___
6. Betty Lou Oliver returned to her work as an elevator operator.	( )	___
7. More people would have been in the building on a weekday.	( )	___

Recognizing Important Details Score [ ]

D — Finding the Main Idea

	Answer	Score
Mark the *main idea*	(**M**)	10
Mark the statement that is *too broad*	(**B**)	5
Mark the statement that is *too narrow*	(**N**)	5

	Answer	Score
1. Three in a plane, plus eleven in the building, died when a bomber crashed into the Empire State Building.	( )	___
2. A number of people died when a plane crashed into a New York City skyscraper.	( )	___
3. Fourteen people died when a bomber crashed into the Empire State Building.	( )	___

Finding the Main Idea Score [ ]

The sight of the Hagenbeck-Wallace Circus Train pulling into a local station had long been a source of delight to adults and children alike. But a series of unfortunate coincidences turned this happy sight into a vision of destruction and death.

94

14

The Circus Troupe's Last Performance

Read this article well enough so that you can answer questions about it. Your teacher may want you to keep track of your reading time. If so, write your reading time on the SCORECARD on page 97 after you finish the article.

Then answer the questions about the article to find out how well you understood what you read. These questions will help you sharpen your reading and thinking skills.

During World War I, the Hagenbeck-Wallace Circus was one of the world's largest tent shows. On the night of June 22, 1918, the show was traveling from Michigan City, Indiana, to Hammond, Indiana. The circus moved with fourteen flatcars carrying tents and equipment, seven animal cars, and four sleepers for the show folk. The sleepers were old-fashioned Pullman cars, built of wood and lit by gas lamps. In the sleeping cars, which were hitched to the very end of the train, were 300 circus people: clowns, acrobats, animal trainers, jugglers and dancers. There was Nellie Jewel, the famous animal trainer; Hercules Navarro, the strongman; and Joe Coyle, the famous

clown. Coyle's family had been complaining that they missed him when he traveled with the circus. So, as a special treat, Coyle's wife and children had joined him for a while. The children were overjoyed by the double thrill of seeing their father and getting to travel on the circus train.

As the train sped through the night, the crew became aware of an overheated brake box and decided to fix it. The train was passing through the town of Ivanhoe, Indiana, which had a railroad yard. The circus train pulled off the main track and into a short track used for switching. The train was so long, however, that the last four cars—the Pullman sleeper cars holding the performers—extended back onto the main track.

The flagman of the circus train, Ernest Trimm, wasn't the least bit worried about the four Pullmans extending out onto the main track. Trimm set emergency flares back down the tracks and checked to be sure that the automatic signal lights shone red. Even without these precautions, however, there should have been no problem. No train was due to come down the track for more than an hour—more than enough time for the circus train's

crew to repair the brake box and get the train on its way.

What Trimm had no way of knowing was that a special train was even then approaching. World War I was responsible for troop trains moving everywhere, carrying soldiers to training camps and to ships leaving for Europe. Alonzo K. Sargent, the engineer of the troop train, was exhausted. He had been shuttling troop trains between New York and Chicago for three days. Sargent also had been suffering from a kidney ailment and had been taking kidney pills that contained a mild pain killer.

On that June evening in 1918, Engineer Sargent's troop train had pulled out of the station early and was rolling down the track toward Ivanhoe, Indiana. Sargent was sound asleep at the throttle. He passed through three yellow caution signals without even slowing down. Sargent's fire tender, beside him in the locomotive's cab, was bent low over the firebox, feeding the boiler. He, too, failed to see the caution signals.

Flagman Trimm of the circus train, was back down the track behind his train. Trimm couldn't believe his eyes as he saw the troop train bearing down toward the circus train. He watched in disbelief as the approaching locomotive ran the three caution lights. Then, Trimm's disbelief turned to horror as the troop train, without slackening its pace, passed through a red stop signal—and kept right on going. Trimm waved his red lantern frantically. Then in a last, desperate effort, he heaved it through the engineer's window of the speeding locomotive. The thrown lantern had no effect on the sleeping engineer.

The locomotive plowed in rapid succession through the wooden sides of the first, second, third and fourth sleeper cars of the circus train. The wooden Pullmans shattered, and the old-fashioned gas lights started fires in the wreckage.

More than eighty-five people died, most of them as the result of burns. Fifty-three badly burned bodies, only three of them identifiable, were buried in a single mass grave. Strongman Hercules Navarro was alive but paralyzed as a result of the crash. Clown Joe Coyle lived through the accident, but his wife and children died.

Panic broke out among the people of the nearby town of Ivanhoe, where the people believed that wild animals had escaped from their circus cages. Rumors claimed that lions and tigers were running wild through the streets. The truth, however, was that most of the animals had been in the forward section of the train, which had not been affected by the wreck. A few animals had been killed in the crash, and police later had to destroy a few other animals that had been painfully injured in the crash.

Some time after the accident, Engineer Sargent was brought to trial. One of the most damaging points against the engineer was the tale told by his fire tender. Right after the crash, the fire tender had run up and down the wreckage shouting, "The engineer was asleep! The engineer was asleep!" Engineer Sargent was, nevertheless, judged to be not guilty.

On the evening after the wreck, the circus opened on schedule. Circus performers and acts from all over the country rushed to Indiana and substituted for dead and injured performers.

Truckloads of flowers from show people all over the country arrived at the circus grounds. An entire vanload of blooms arrived from the great entertainer George M. Cohan. But the flower that was best remembered was a single rose. It came from a child who had seen the show just before the crash. The card that came with the flower read: "From a little girl who laughed at your show and now cries for you." ■

Find out your reading time and enter it on the SCORECARD. Then turn to page 157 and look up your reading speed. Write the Words per Minute on the SCORECARD.

Now go on to the exercises in "How Well Did You Read?" Use the SCORECARD to record your critical reading scores. When the SCORECARD is full, transfer your Words per Minute and Critical Reading Score to the graphs on pages 158 and 159.

SCORECARD

Reading Speed

Reading Time _____ : _____
                     Minutes Seconds

Words per Minute [   ]

How Well Did You Read?

Using Words Precisely   ____

Choosing the Best Title   ____

Recognizing Important Details ____

Finding the Main Idea   ____

Critical Reading Score [   ]
(Add the 4 scores above)

14. The Circus Troupe's Last Performance

How Well Did You Read?

Answer the four types of questions that follow. The directions for each type of question tell you how to mark and score your answers.

After you have answered all the questions, check your work using the Answer Key on page 151. If you have the right answer, write the score on the gray line next to the answer. If your answer is wrong, write 0 on the line.

Then add your scores for each type of question and write the total scores in the gray brackets. Enter the four total scores on the SCORECARD and add them to find your Critical Reading Score.

A Using Words Precisely

	Answer	Score
Mark the word or phrase that has the *same* meaning as the underlined word	(S)	3
Mark the word or phrase that has *almost the same* meaning as the underlined word	(A)	1
Mark the word or phrase that is the *opposite* of the underlined word	(O)	1

	Answer	Score

1. Even without these <u>precautions</u>, however, there should have been no problem.

   a. safeguards   ( ) ____

   b. dangers   ( ) ____

   c. extra steps   ( ) ____

2. The engineer had been <u>shuttling</u> troop trains between New York and Chicago for three days.

   a. sending away   ( ) ____

   b. sending back and forth ( ) ____

   c. keeping in one place   ( ) ____

A — Using Words Precisely (continued)

Answer   Score

3. The troop train, without <u>slackening</u> its pace, passed through a red stop signal.

   a. speeding up   ( ) ___

   b. changing speed   ( ) ___

   c. going any slower   ( ) ___

4. The locomotive plowed in rapid <u>succession</u> through the wooden sides of the four sleeping cars.

   a. all at once   ( ) ___

   b. one after the other ( ) ___

   c. in definite order   ( ) ___

5. The sleeping cars were <u>hitched</u> to the very end of the train.

   a. held against   ( ) ___

   b. fastened to   ( ) ___

   c. loosened from   ( ) ___

Using Words Precisely Score   [ ]

B — Choosing the Best Title

Answer   Score

Mark the *best title* .... (T)   __10__

Mark the title that is *too broad* .... (B)   __5__

Mark the title that is *too narrow* .... (N)   __5__

Answer   Score

1. Wreck of the Hagenbeck-Wallace Circus Train   ( ) ___

2. Circus Train   ( ) ___

3. Train Wreck at Ivanhoe, Indiana   ( ) ___

Choosing the Best Title Score   [ ]

C — Recognizing Important Details

	Answer	Score
Mark the details that are *true*	(**T**)	5
Mark the details that are *false*	(**F**)	5
Mark the details that are *not mentioned* in the article	(**N**)	5

	Answer	Score
1. The circus train was wrecked during World War II.	( )	___
2. Joe Coyle's children wanted to be circus clowns like their famous father.	( )	___
3. The circus train stopped to repair a brake box.	( )	___
4. The circus train was too long to fit on the short, switching track.	( )	___
5. The accident might have been avoided if Flagman Trimm had set up signal flares down the track.	( )	___
6. The fire tender of the troop train had been asleep until just before the accident.	( )	___
7. Entertainer George M. Cohan sent a single rose.	( )	___

Recognizing Important Details Score [ ]

D — Finding the Main Idea

	Answer	Score
Mark the *main idea*	(**M**)	10
Mark the statement that is *too broad*	(**B**)	5
Mark the statement that is *too narrow*	(**N**)	5

	Answer	Score
1. A circus train wreck involved a tragic loss of life.	( )	___
2. Clown Joe Coyle lived through the wreck of a circus train that wiped out his family.	( )	___
3. A sleeping engineer ran his locomotive into a circus train, killing dozens of performers.	( )	___

Finding the Main Idea Score [ ]

Group Three

"Bring out your dead," shouted the town crier as huge numbers of bodies were piled onto burial carts. In the 1300s, the Black Death killed one out of every three people, and neither religion nor medicine seemed capable of halting its advance across all of Europe. People feared it was the end of the world.

15

Black Death: The End of the World

Read this article well enough so that you can answer questions about it. Your teacher may want you to keep track of your reading time. If so, write your reading time on the SCORECARD on page 105 after you finish the article.

Then answer the questions about the article to find out how well you understood what you read. These questions will help you sharpen your reading and thinking skills.

"Bring out your dead! Bring out your dead!" the driver cried as the horse-drawn carts rumbled through the streets of Europe in the 1300s. Bodies were dragged from almost every house and thrown onto the carts. Corpse was tossed on top of corpse until they were like logs in a pile of firewood. Sometimes several bodies were carried out of the same house. The Black Death had struck! One person in every three would die of the plague before it ran its course.

The Black Death was the worst calamity of all times, wiping out the entire populations of some villages. In the large city of Smolensk, Russia, only five people survived the plague. Nine out of every ten citizens of London fell victim to the Black Death. Virtually the entire populations of Iceland and Cyprus were wiped out.

So many people were struck down by the plague, that the supply of coffins was soon exhausted, and the dead were carried on wooden planks to huge mass-burial pits. Corpses were piled several high, and then a thin layer of dirt was shoveled over them. Often the burials took place with no member of the family or clergy present. As people fled before the spreading plague, spouse abandoned spouse, and parents forsook children.

The plague spread quickly from person to person. People went to bed well and were dead by morning. A doctor might arrive at a home to treat a victim only to catch the plague and die before the original sufferer.

The Black Death derived its name from the color of the victim's skin in death; a person who was infected always died within three days, skin covered by black patches. There were other symptoms too. Patients developed egg-size swellings in the groin and arm pits. Sometimes victims also coughed and sweated violently.

The first people to know the horror of the Black Death were the Chinese, who were hit by the plague earlier in the fourteenth century. The disease quickly spread to the Tartars, a people originally from the area where the present-day borders of China and the Soviet Union meet. The Tartars, under their great leader Kipchak Janiberg, had fought their way westward across Russia. They had conquered all the Russian lands as far into Europe as the Black Sea—but they carried the plague with them.

The Tartar advance had been halted by a trading colony of Italians located in a city on the Black Sea. As more and more of Kipchak's Tartars became victims of the Black Death, he began to realize that the Italian city would never fall to him. Kipchak's troops had brought huge *catapults*, devices like giant slingshots, with them. The Tartars used them for throwing huge stones against the stone walls of forts. Kipchak had the catapults loaded with the bodies of Tartars who had died of the Black Death. The corpses were thrown over the walls and into the city, where they quickly spread the plague to the Italian colonists.

Both Italians and Tartars abandoned the city. Some of the Italians boarded a galley and rowed to Italy as fast as they could. When the galley arrived at the

Italian port of Messina, the inhabitants of the port found some of the rowers dead and the remainder dying of the plague. The Black Death had come to Italy.

The plague quickly spread throughout Italy and passed on to France. From France, the plague was carried across the English Channel to Great Britain. The cycle of death was completed when the plague spread from Britain to all the rest of Europe, sparing no country. Human survival was threatened. No wonder people said,—and believed—"This is the end of the world."

Many people believed that the plague was caused by the wrath of God. Societies of *flagellants* formed. The societies derived their name from the whips members used to beat themselves and each other. Dressed in sackcloth and ashes, the flagellants moved from town to town, beating themselves with leather whips tipped with metal points.

The flagellation made as much sense as some of the other cures proposed for the plague. The crude science of the fourteenth century gave no idea of either the cause of the Black Death or its cure. Thinkers came up with an idea that combined astrology, geology and superstition. Jupiter and Mars had passed very close to Earth and the proximity of the two planets was believed to have caused

cracks in the earth's crust. The cracks, they believed, permitted poisonous fumes from the earth's center to escape and cause the plague.

Since the scientists of the time had no idea of the plague's cause, their "cures" were nearly as horrible as the disease itself. People ate and drank concoctions of blood, goat urine, lizards, toads, and boils that had been dried and powdered. Plague victims were advised to rip open the bodies of puppies and pigeons and hold the torn flesh against their plague boils. While people were vainly trying these cures, the Black Death continued its deadly passage across Europe.

The real cause of the plague had been partially discovered by an Arab physician four hundred years before. The physician had noted that the plague broke out only after rats had come out of their holes to die in the open air. This observation was accurate, but failed to take into account one final piece needed for the puzzle's solution—fleas. The plague germs lived and multiplied in the bodies of fleas. Every rat had hundreds of fleas which lived on rats' blood and infected them with the Black Death. When the rats died of the plague, the fleas jumped onto the nearest people. It was the bite of the fleas that spread the plague germs to their human victims.

There were house rats in every fourteenth-century city, so nobody was spared. The Black Death carried off king and commoner alike. It raged back and forth over Europe, on and off, for 200 years. Then gradually, it died away. (Some people think that the real end of the plague didn't come until the London Fire of 1666. This fire destroyed most of London, along with the rats, fleas and germs that caused the plague.)

Surprisingly, during all the 200 years that the plague circled back and forth across Europe, the cure had been at hand. The germs of the Black Death can be destroyed by the application of soap and water. ■

Find out your reading time and enter it on the SCORECARD. Then turn to page 157 and look up your reading speed. Write the Words per Minute on the SCORECARD.

Now go on to the exercises in "How Well Did You Read?" Use the SCORE-CARD to record your critical reading scores. When the SCORECARD is full, transfer your Words per Minute and Critical Reading Score to the graphs on pages 158 and 159.

SCORECARD

Reading Speed

Reading Time _____ : _____
                    Minutes   Seconds

Words per Minute **[   ]**

How Well Did You Read?

Using Words Precisely _____

Choosing the Best Title _____

Recognizing Important Details _____

Finding the Main Idea _____

Critical Reading Score **[   ]**
(Add the 4 scores above)

15. Black Death: The End of the World

How Well Did You Read?

Answer the four types of questions that follow. The directions for each type of question tell you how to mark and score your answers.

After you have answered all the questions, check your work using the Answer Key on page 151. If you have the right answer, write the score on the gray line next to the answer. If your answer is wrong, write 0 on the line.

Then add your scores for each type of question and write the total scores in the gray brackets. Enter the four total scores on the SCORECARD and add them to find your Critical Reading Score.

A — Using Words Precisely

	Answer	Score
Mark the word or phrase that has the *same* meaning as the underlined word	(**S**)	3
Mark the word or phrase that has *almost the same* meaning as the underlined word	(**A**)	1
Mark the word or phrase that is the *opposite* of the underlined word	(**O**)	1

	Answer	Score
1. One person in every three would die before the plague <u>ran its course</u>.		
a. started to occur	( )	___
b. continued for a long time	( )	___
c. came to an end	( )	___
2. Virtually the entire populations of Iceland and Cyprus were <u>wiped out</u>.		
a. weakened	( )	___
b. eliminated	( )	___
c. increased	( )	___

A Using Words Precisely (continued)

Answer   Score

3. As people fled before the spreading plague, parents <u>forsook</u> children.

   a. deserted   ( ) ___

   b. came to   ( ) ___

   c. departed from   ( ) ___

4. The Black Death <u>derived</u> its name from the color of the victim's skin in death.

   a. received   ( ) ___

   b. gave up   ( ) ___

   c. copied   ( ) ___

5. A physician <u>noted</u> that the plague broke out only after rats came out of their holes and died.

   a. failed to see   ( ) ___

   b. knew   ( ) ___

   c. realized   ( ) ___

Using Words Precisely Score [ ]

B Choosing the Best Title

Answer   Score

Mark the *best title* .... (T)   __10__

Mark the title that is *too broad* .... (B)   __5__

Mark the title that is *too narrow* .... (N)   __5__

Answer   Score

1. Deadly Plague   ( ) ___

2. One in Three Died   ( ) ___

3. The Black Death   ( ) ___

Choosing the Best Title Score [ ]

C — Recognizing Important Details

	Answer	Score
Mark the details that are *true*	(**T**)	5
Mark the details that are *false*	(**F**)	5
Mark the details that are *not mentioned* in the article	(**N**)	5

	Answer	Score
1. The Black Death wiped out the whole populations of some villages.	( )	___
2. The Chinese brought the plague to Smolensk, Russia.	( )	___
3. When no member of the clergy was present at the funeral, gravediggers said the prayers.	( )	___
4. The people of China started to fall victim to the Black Death after they were weakened by a long famine.	( )	___
5. Kipchak had the bodies of his own soldiers thrown at his enemies.	( )	___
6. The relationship between the Black Death and fleas had been noted by an Arab physician years before the plague struck Europe.	( )	___
7. The Black Death circled back and forth across Europe for 200 years.	( )	___

Recognizing Important Details Score [ ]

D — Finding the Main Idea

	Answer	Score
Mark the *main idea*	(**M**)	10
Mark the statement that is *too broad*	(**B**)	5
Mark the statement that is *too narrow*	(**N**)	5

	Answer	Score
1. Millions of people died of the plague known as the Black Death.	( )	___
2. The Black Death, which killed millions of people in the fourteenth century, was spread by fleas.	( )	___
3. Some people believed that the Black Death was caused by poisonous fumes escaping from the center of the earth.	( )	___

Finding the Main Idea Score [ ]

16

The Great Chicago Fire

Read this article well enough so that you can answer questions about it. Your teacher may want you to keep track of your reading time. If so, write your reading time on the SCORECARD on page 111 after you finish the article.

Then answer the questions about the article to find out how well you understood what you read. These questions will help you sharpen your reading and thinking skills.

There is an old song about how Mrs. O'Leary's cow started the Chicago Fire and it is probably true. The O'Leary family, however, has always claimed that the fire was started by a group of boys who were smoking in the barn. One thing is certain: the biggest and worst human-made disaster in North American history started in the O'Leary barn.

In 1871, Patrick and Catherine O'Leary lived on Chicago's West Side. Patrick made a poor living carrying heavy loads by hand. Catherine added to their income with a dairy business of her own. She kept five cows in the barn behind their house, and sold their milk to other families in the neighborhood.

Late in the evening of October 8, 1871, fire broke out in the O'Leary barn. According to the story told by Daniel Sullivan, the O'Learys' peg-legged neighbor, the villain was the cow who kicked over the kerosene lantern.

The hero of the story Sullivan told is—Daniel Sullivan. He rushed into the barn to try to save the cows. He managed to—although he almost fell victim to the fire himself. When Sullivan had led some of the cows to safety, the tip of his peg leg became stuck in a crack in the barn's wooden floor. As the flames closed in, Sullivan managed to pull loose barely in time to save the remaining cows—and his own life.

The Chicago Fire turned out to be so great a catastrophe not because of Mrs. O'Leary's cow, but because of the way Chicago itself was built and managed. The city had 651 miles of wooden sidewalks. There were 60,000 buildings—most of them constructed of wood. In the midst of all this wood, the fire department had 17 horse-drawn steam pumpers and 18 hook-and-ladder trucks. Although Chicago had a population of 350,000, the fire department had a force of only 200.

The night the Great Fire broke out, Chicago's fire fighters were dead tired.

They had faced thirty fires during the week before, and the last fire had been an especially bad one. The fire fighters had drunk a lot of whiskey after that blaze, and many of them had hangovers. Later, some critics were to claim that many fire fighters were still drunk when the big fire broke out.

The fire department's central headquarters was located in the city's stone "fireproof" courthouse. A fire lookout atop the courthouse's tall tower spotted smoke from the fire at the O'Leary barn and sent in the alarm. Unfortunately, the lookout reported the wrong location. By the time the correct location was discovered, the fire had gotten a solid start. The fire spread—out of control—forcing citizens to flee their homes, and driving everyone, including the fire department, before it. The fire fighters fought back bravely, but they had little to fight with.

The wooden buildings and sidewalks gave off millions of flying sparks, some of them the size of baseballs. And the winds resulting from the fires drove those fireballs as far as well-hit baseballs. The fireballs crossed streets and jumped over buildings and across the river, spreading the blaze.

Chicago was a thriving commercial center when the Great Fire broke out. By the time the last flame was extinguished, the city, built almost entirely of wood, looked like an ancient ruin, and at least 300 people were dead.

The fire raced on. Racing before it were the looters, drunk with liquor from the saloons and stores they'd broken into. Merchants and homeowners who tried to protect their possessions were struck down—even killed. The fire moved toward Chicago's "fireproof" courthouse. Although the building was faced with a layer of limestone and its interior was marble, the heat of the fire was too intense, even for stone, and the courthouse started to go. The basement of the building housed the city's jail, where dozens of prisoners were locked up and screaming to be released. A police captain ordered the police to take the murderers outside and keep them under guard there. All other prisoners were freed.

The convicts ran down the street, unable to believe their good fortune. Their fortune really improved when they reached a well-known jewelry store. The store was already smoldering. The store's owner held out his hands to the convicts. In them he held rings, necklaces and bracelets. "Help yourselves, gentlemen," he called. The jeweler realized that if the convicts didn't get the goods, the fire would. It made little difference to him whether the jewelry was stolen by convicts

or melted by the fire. The jeweler, A. H. Miller, picked out a few of his most valuable gems and walked away with them.

People trapped in the second and third floors of houses with bottom floors on fire threw their most precious possessions to others gathered in the street. One woman dropped a large bundle of bed-sheets to a man waiting below her windows. The woman quickly followed her belongings through the window when she saw the man run off with the bundle. The bundle contained the woman's baby. The screaming mother pursued the thief as he cut in and out among the crowd, fleeing across a bridge leading from the burning city. Thief and bundle disappeared in the mass of people. The heartsick mother was thinking of leaping to her death over the railing of the bridge when she spotted her baby. He was alive, lying on some bales of cotton ten feet below. The mother climbed down the bridge's steelwork and retrieved her infant.

The rest of Chicago did not get off so luckily. Its doom was sealed by a single burning plank carried aloft by the power-ful, hot winds stirred up by the blaze. The burning plank sailed through the air until it reached the waterworks, where it crashed through the wooden roof. The waterworks had been considered fireproof, but its wooden ceiling was soon on fire. The ceiling fell onto the pumps that supplied the city with water, and put them out of action. The fire fighters, left without water, were forced to give up the battle.

The fire burned out of control for thirty hours, until the early morning of October 10, 1871. Then, the wind died down and it started to rain. The rain was soon spattering onto the cinders and charred wreckage of what had been the city of Chicago. The fire destroyed 200 million dollars worth of buildings and left 100,000 people homeless.

Chicagoans turned their wrath on Patrick O'Leary. O'Leary, fearing for his life, escaped by dressing as a woman. He hid at a friend's house until the mob's anger died.

Chicago made a fast recovery from the fire. Six months after the blaze, half of the city had been rebuilt. In just a few years there was no sign of the fire, and the population had doubled. Hundreds of the city's new citizens were happy to buy a dramatic souvenir of the Great Fire. Many of Chicago's old-timers had discovered that they could make money selling the hoof of the cow that kicked over the lantern and started the fire. They sold hundreds of that hoof. ∎

Find out your reading time and enter it on the SCORECARD. Then turn to page 157 and look up your reading speed. Write the Words per Minute on the SCORECARD.

Now go on to the exercises in "How Well Did You Read?" Use the SCORE-CARD to record your critical reading scores. When the SCORECARD is full, transfer your Words per Minute and Critical Reading Score to the graphs on pages 158 and 159.

SCORECARD

Reading Speed

Reading Time ____ : ____

Minutes Seconds

Words per Minute [   ]

How Well Did You Read?

Using Words Precisely ____

Choosing the Best Title ____

Recognizing Important Details ____

Finding the Main Idea ____

Critical Reading Score [   ]
(Add the 4 scores above)

16. The Great Chicago Fire

How Well Did You Read?

Answer the four types of questions that follow. The directions for each type of question tell you how to mark and score your answers.

After you have answered all the questions, check your work using the Answer Key on page 152. If you have the right answer, write the score on the gray line next to the answer. If your answer is wrong, write 0 on the line.

Then add your scores for each type of question and write the total scores in the gray brackets. Enter the four total scores on the SCORECARD and add them to find your Critical Reading Score.

A Using Words Precisely

	Answer	Score
Mark the word or phrase that has the *same* meaning as the underlined word	(S)	3
Mark the word or phrase that has *almost the same* meaning as the underlined word	(A)	1
Mark the word or phrase that is the *opposite* of the underlined word	(O)	1

	Answer	Score
1. The store was already <u>smoldering</u>.		
a. about to go up in flames	( )	___
b. smoking after a blaze died down	( )	___
c. fireproof and incapable of burning	( )	___
2. The screaming mother <u>pursued</u> the thief.		
a. chased	( )	___
b. followed	( )	___
c. let go	( )	___

A — Using Words Precisely (continued)

Answer Score

3. The mother climbed down and <u>retrieved</u> her infant.

   a. lost   ( ) ___

   b. claimed   ( ) ___

   c. recovered   ( ) ___

4. O'Leary hid until the anger of the <u>mob</u> died.

   a. large crowd   ( ) ___

   b. well-mannered group   ( ) ___

   c. disorderly crowd   ( ) ___

5. Chicagoans turned their <u>wrath</u> on Patrick O'Leary.

   a. fury or rage   ( ) ___

   b. anger   ( ) ___

   c. affection   ( ) ___

Using Words Precisely Score **[ ]**

B — Choosing the Best Title

Answer Score

Mark the *best title* .... (T) __10__

Mark the title that is *too broad* .... (B) __5__

Mark the title that is *too narrow* .... (N) __5__

Answer Score

1. Mrs. O'Leary's Cow   ( ) ___

2. City on Fire   ( ) ___

3. The Fire That Destroyed Chicago   ( ) ___

Choosing the Best Title Score **[ ]**

C — Recognizing Important Details

	Answer	Score
Mark the details that are *true*	(T)	5
Mark the details that are *false*	(F)	5
Mark the details that are *not mentioned* in the article	(N)	5

	Answer	Score
1. Patrick O'Leary's peg leg got stuck in the floor when he led his cows to safety.	( )	__
2. Chicago had an unusually large fire department.	( )	__
3. A fire spotter reported the wrong location for the O'Leary barn.	( )	__
4. Sparks from the fire were as large as basketballs.	( )	__
5. All prisoners in the courthouse jail, except murderers, were freed.	( )	__
6. Jeweler A. H. Miller rebuilt an even bigger store after the fire.	( )	__
7. It was rain, rather than the fire department, that finally put out the fire.	( )	__

Recognizing Important Details Score [ ]

D — Finding the Main Idea

	Answer	Score
Mark the *main idea*	(M)	10
Mark the statement that is *too broad*	(B)	5
Mark the statement that is *too narrow*	(N)	5

	Answer	Score
1. Chicago was the scene of the greatest human-made disaster in North America.	( )	__
2. Thousands of people were left homeless when fire destroyed nineteenth-century Chicago.	( )	__
3. The fire that destroyed Chicago was started at the O'Leary barn on Chicago's West Side.	( )	__

Finding the Main Idea Score [ ]

The *Lusitania*, seen here in port, was an admired British luxury liner often used by citizens of the United States. One of the events that forced the United States into World War I was the sinking of the *Lusitania* by a German submarine. A total of 1,198 people, more than 100 of them United States citizens, went down with the British liner. Who is to blame for their deaths: the Germans? the British? or the victims themselves?

17

The Sinking of the *Lusitania*

Read this article well enough so that you can answer questions about it. Your teacher may want you to keep track of your reading time. If so, write your reading time on the SCORECARD on page 117 after you finish the article.

Then answer the questions about the article to find out how well you understood what you read. These questions will help you sharpen your reading and thinking skills.

It had been a good war cruise for German Navy officer Walter Schwieger and the crew of his U-boat. The U-20 had already sunk three British ships and had only two torpedoes left. Now Schwieger had the biggest prize of all in the cross hairs of his periscope—a big, fat luxury liner. Lieutenant Schwieger carefully checked the angle for a torpedo shot. He then gave the order, "Fire!"

The torpedo ran straight and true. Aboard the large ship, a passenger watched in disbelief as the torpedo approached, churning the water in front of it. As the foaming white feather bore in on the liner, the passenger turned to the next person and asked, "Is that a torpedo?"

A crew member on watch didn't have to wonder what the approaching string of air bubbles meant. The sailor called, "Torpedo coming in on starboard side!"

There was an explosion like the sound of a steel door slamming shut as the torpedo ploughed into the *Lusitania*'s Number 1 and Number 2 boilers. Two minutes later, there was a second explosion. This one sounded like a dull thud. The *Lusitania* listed to starboard and began to sink by the head.

Lieutenant Schwieger did not know that the ship he had just fired on was the *Lusitania*. Schwieger did know that he was operating in British waters. And he knew that British warships might attack at any minute. He felt he had time for just one quick look-around before British rescue ships would begin to arrive. Schwieger ran up his periscope. He made out the name on the now-sinking ship, then quickly gave orders to dive and head for Germany. Later, Schwieger described to his fellow officers the sight of the sinking ship. "The scene was too horrible to watch," he said.

That horrible scene was the death of 1,198 of the 1,918 people aboard the *Lusitania*.

The *Lusitania*'s torpedoing did not come as a complete surprise to its captain or passengers. World War I had been raging for a year. Germany had announced that it intended to carry on unrestricted submarine warfare. It claimed the right to destroy any British ship carrying war supplies to Britain. In fact, shortly before the *Lusitania* sailed, New York newspapers had carried a German advertisement warning United States citizens of the danger of sailing on British ships. The ad was signed and paid for by the Imperial German Embassy in Washington, D.C. It warned its readers not to enter the war zone aboard a British ship.

Despite the ad, 197 United States citizens boarded the *Lusitania* in New York City for a trip to Liverpool, England. For many years, people from the United States had been in the habit of traveling aboard British ships. They didn't intend to stop because of the World War. The United States wasn't involved in that war. Besides, the *Lusitania* was strictly a passenger ship. Surely, United States citizens reasoned, the Germans wouldn't sink a ship that had hundreds of women and children aboard, and did not carry war cargo.

Captain Will Turner of the *Lusitania* had reason to believe that the Germans might strike, however. He had just received a wireless message from the British Admiralty. The cable stated, "Submarines active off the coast of Ireland." The message failed to indicate just how active the subs were. In the six days since the *Lusitania* had sailed from New York, German U-boats had sunk twenty-three subs near the Irish coast.

Captain Turner ordered the lifeboats made ready but there was little else that he could do. Will Turner was a perfect sea captain. He had first gone to sea as a thirteen-year-old cabin boy. He had worked his way up through the ranks to command the world's finest passenger ship.

After the torpedo struck, Captain Turner waited and made certain that there was no chance to save his vessel before giving it up. Then he gave the two ancient calls of the sea: "Abandon ship," and then, "Women and children first!"

Not all of the *Lusitania*'s crew were experienced at sea. Many of them were new to both the ship and to the sea. A large part of the *Lusitania*'s regular crew were members of the naval reserve. They had been called to active warship service at the start of the war. The inexperienced

sailors were having real trouble. The steep angle of the *Lusitania*'s list made it difficult for the crew to get the boats into the water. Only one lifeboat out of every eight that the *Lusitania* carried reached shore. A total of 1,198 people died. Of these, 94 were children. Of the 197 people from the United States aboard the *Lusitania*, 128 lost their lives.

Britain branded the *Lusitania*'s sinking a savage act. Germany claimed that it was fighting for its life. The German government stated that it was necessary to sink British ships that were supplying Britain with war goods. Britain, of course, denied that the *Lusitania* carried any war cargo. The United States, which was neutral at the time, treated the taking of United States lives as an unforgivable outrage. An advisor to the president, commenting on the *Lusitania*'s sinking, stated, "War with Germany is inevitable." The inevitable came in less than two years. The sinking of the *Lusitania* was, perhaps, the single most important event leading the United States to enter World War I.

Was the *Lusitania* carrying war goods as Germany claimed? Had the U-boat fired two torpedoes as the British maintained? Or had the second explosion aboard the *Lusitania* been the blowing up of the munitions it was carrying? It seemed for years that the answers would

lie forever under 250 feet of water. Then in 1950, thirty-five years after the *Lusitania* went down, the British government released a list of the cargo carried by the great liner. The list showed, quite clearly, that the *Lusitania*'s cargo included cartridges and other war material. ■

A view of some survivors of the sinking of the *Lusitania*.

Find out your reading time and enter it on the SCORECARD. Then turn to page 157 and look up your reading speed. Write the Words per Minute on the SCORECARD.

Now go on to the exercises in "How Well Did You Read?" Use the SCORECARD to record your critical reading scores. When the SCORECARD is full, transfer your Words per Minute and Critical Reading Score to the graphs on pages 158 and 159.

SCORECARD

Reading Speed

Reading Time _____ : _____
          Minutes   Seconds

Words per Minute [   ]

How Well Did You Read?

Using Words Precisely _____

Choosing the Best Title _____

Recognizing Important Details _____

Finding the Main Idea _____

Critical Reading Score [   ]
(Add the 4 scores above)

17. The Sinking of the *Lusitania*

How Well Did You Read?

Answer the four types of questions that follow. The directions for each type of question tell you how to mark and score your answers.

After you have answered all the questions, check your work using the Answer Key on page 152. If you have the right answer, write the score on the gray line next to the answer. If your answer is wrong, write 0 on the line.

Then add your scores for each type of question and write the total scores in the gray brackets. Enter the four total scores on the SCORECARD and add them to find your Critical Reading Score.

A Using Words Precisely

	Answer	Score
Mark the word or phrase that has the *same* meaning as the underlined word	(S)	3
Mark the word or phrase that has *almost the same* meaning as the underlined word	(A)	1
Mark the word or phrase that is the *opposite* of the underlined word	(O)	1

	Answer	Score
1. Germany had announced that it intended to carry on <u>unrestricted</u> submarine warfare.		
a. operating within certain rules	( )	___
b. not confined to	( )	___
c. not bound by any rules	( )	___
2. Captain Turner gave the ancient call of the sea, "<u>Abandon</u> ship."		
a. leave for a time	( )	___
b. leave permanently	( )	___
c. stay on board	( )	___

A — Using Words Precisely (continued)

Answer   Score

3. Britain <u>branded</u> the *Lusitania's* sinking a savage act.

    a. called   ( ) ___

    b. labeled as shameful   ( ) ___

    c. covered up   ( ) ___

4. That <u>horrible</u> scene was the death of 1,198 of the 1,918 people aboard the *Lusitania*.

    a. terrible   ( ) ___

    b. depressing   ( ) ___

    c. wonderful   ( ) ___

5. Had the second explosion aboard the *Lusitania* been the blowing up of <u>munitions</u>?

    a. explosives and ammunition   ( ) ___

    b. supplies for the soldiers   ( ) ___

    c. peacetime merchandise   ( ) ___

Using Words Precisely Score **[ ]**

B — Choosing the Best Title

Answer   Score

Mark the *best title* .... (**T**)   <u>10</u>

Mark the title that is *too broad* .... (**B**)   <u>5</u>

Mark the title that is *too narrow* .... (**N**)   <u>5</u>

Answer   Score

1. U-Boat Attack   ( ) ___

2. Sinking the *Lusitania* leads the U.S. to War   ( ) ___

3. Munitions On Board the *Lusitania*   ( ) ___

Choosing the Best Title Score **[ ]**

C — Recognizing Important Details

	Answer	Score
Mark the details that are *true*	(T)	5
Mark the details that are *false*	(F)	5
Mark the details that are *not mentioned* in the article	(N)	5

	Answer	Score
1. Lieutenant Schwieger knew the ship he was firing on was the *Lusitania*.	( )	___
2. Germany had announced unrestricted submarine warfare in newspapers all over the world.	( )	___
3. The *Lusitania* was sailing for Ireland when it was torpedoed.	( )	___
4. Captain Turner waited for a while before giving the order to abandon ship.	( )	___
5. Most of the *Lusitania*'s crew members were experienced sailors.	( )	___
6. A presidential adviser felt that the *Lusitania*'s sinking would bring the U.S. into the war.	( )	___
7. The *Lusitania* had been carrying munitions, as the Germans always claimed.	( )	___

Recognizing Important Details Score [ ]

D — Finding the Main Idea

	Answer	Score
Mark the *main idea*	(M)	10
Mark the statement that is *too broad*	(B)	5
Mark the statement that is *too narrow*	(N)	5

	Answer	Score
1. A German submarine attacked the *Lusitania*.	( )	___
2. Many passengers, U.S. citizens among them, lost their lives when a U-boat sank the *Lusitania*.	( )	___
3. German U-boats operating off the Irish coast sank twenty-four ships.	( )	___

Finding the Main Idea Score [ ]

The New London, Texas, Consolidated School was located in the middle of one of the world's richest oil fields. Despite this fact, the townspeople tried to save money by heating the school with raw natural gas. They saved the money—but it cost them the lives of 419 students and teachers. Faulty equipment allowed the dangerous raw gas to fill the entire building, resulting in a huge explosion that blew the roof off the school and caused the walls to crumble.

18

Penny-Pinching Brings Death at the World's Richest School

Read this article well enough so that you can answer questions about it. Your teacher may want you to keep track of your reading time. If so, write your reading time on the SCORECARD on page 123 after you finish the article.

Then answer the questions about the article to find out how well you understood what you read. These questions will help you sharpen your reading and thinking skills.

People in Texas claimed that the New London Consolidated School was the world's wealthiest school. It was located in the midst of the world's richest oil field. The two-story brick building served pupils from kindergarten through grade twelve. From the school, the students could see a forest of oil wells and derricks. By night, the school was lit by the flare of the extra gas from the wells burning off in the air. This same gas was used to heat the Consolidated School, which had no central heating system. Each of the school's radiators burned the gas known as *wet gas* that came directly from the wells.

The *wet gas* saved the school the $250 to $300 per month it would have cost to heat the school with the regular household gas that many homes use for cooking and heating. *Wet gas*, however, has several serious disadvantages. It is very uneven in composition, so any equipment that uses *wet gas* has to be in perfect running order. Unfortunately, not all the radiators at the Consolidated School were in good order. And, because *wet gas* doesn't have the characteristic smell of regular household gas, its presence is undetectable.

Certainly nobody was aware of the gas building up in every corner of every room of the Consolidated School that late afternoon of March 18, 1937. The school day was already over for almost all the pupils in the elementary grades. Students in grades seven through twelve still had another quarter of an hour of school. It was only by a stroke of bad luck that any students were in school at all. School officials had considered closing school a half hour early so that students could attend a track meet. As it turned out, school was not closed, and 690 students were still in the building when tragedy struck.

At 3:15 P.M., there was a long, rumbling explosion and the New London, Texas, Consolidated School blew up.

The roof lifted, the walls bulged outward, and then, the roof came back down on top of tables, desks, chairs and the students and teachers. A Parent Teacher Association meeting was being held in a gymnasium located about 300 feet from the main part of the school. At the sound of the explosion, the mothers ran toward the main building. The first mothers to rush outside saw bodies flying upward through the air. Then, as the mothers looked on in horror, the bodies fell back into the wreckage of what had once been a school.

There were joyous reunions of the students who had escaped the blast and their mothers. Then, all the mothers attacked the wreckage, clawing at it with their bare hands. Hundreds of workers from the nearby oil fields joined the mothers. They lifted bricks and beams and plaster in response to moans from underneath the wreckage. Then, the rescuers had to slow down their frenzied digging. They were afraid of loosening debris which would drop onto the trapped students.

The rescue work proceeded rapidly but

carefully under huge floodlights set up by the oil field people. A total of 3,000 oil workers used the tools of their trade—acetylene cutting torches and heavy steel cables attached to huge trucks and tractors—to clear away the wreckage. Many of the oil field people were working to rescue their own children. Eighty-five students were freed from the wreckage alive—though two of them died later. Some of the survivors owed their lives to school desks that protected them from falling debris. One student just happened to be bent over, looking for something under her desk, when the roof and walls collapsed. The desk held, allowing rescuers to save her. Another group of survivors owed their lives to a large bookcase that fell against a wall, forming a tunnel that held until rescue workers dug the students out.

One of every three young people of New London, Texas, died in the explosion. There were ninety-two seniors in the graduating high school class. Only one survived. In all, 419 bodies were removed from the school.

The people of New London sought to learn what caused their tragedy, setting up a board of inquiry to sift through the evidence. The board discovered that only one radiator, of the six that survived the blast, was in working order. This led the investigators to conclude that many of the school's radiators had been leaking *wet gas*. A great deal of the gas must have built up in an industrial arts shop. This gas needed only one spark to set it off. That spark came when a shop teacher flicked a wall switch to turn on a machine for a student. (It is not known whether that student was one of those who survived.)

Included in the wreckage of the school was a blackboard on which a teacher had written: *Oil and gas are East Texas's greatest mineral blessings. Without them, this school would not be here and none of us would be learning our lessons.* ■

Find out your reading time and enter it on the SCORECARD. Then turn to page 157 and look up your reading speed. Write the Words per Minute on the SCORECARD.

Now go on to the exercises in "How Well Did You Read?" Use the SCORECARD to record your critical reading scores. When the SCORECARD is full, transfer your Words per Minute and Critical Reading Score to the graphs on pages 158 and 159.

SCORECARD

Reading Speed

Reading Time _____ : _____
Minutes   Seconds

Words per Minute [   ]

How Well Did You Read?

Using Words Precisely _____

Choosing the Best Title _____

Recognizing Important Details _____

Finding the Main Idea _____

Critical Reading Score [   ]
(Add the 4 scores above)

18. Penny-Pinching Brings Death at the World's Richest School

How Well Did You Read?

Answer the four types of questions that follow. The directions for each type of question tell you how to mark and score your answers.

After you have answered all the questions, check your work using the Answer Key on page 152. If you have the right answer, write the score on the gray line next to the answer. If your answer is wrong, write 0 on the line.

Then add your scores for each type of question and write the total scores in the gray brackets. Enter the four total scores on the SCORECARD and add them to find your Critical Reading Score.

A Using Words Precisely

	Answer	Score
Mark the word or phrase that has the *same* meaning as the underlined word	(S)	3
Mark the word or phrase that has *almost the same* meaning as the underlined word	(A)	1
Mark the word or phrase that is the *opposite* of the underlined word	(O)	1

	Answer	Score
1. *Wet gas* is <u>uneven</u> in <u>composition</u>.		
a. consistent throughout	( )	___
b. irregularly arranged	( )	___
c. varying in makeup	( )	___
2. *Wet gas* doesn't have the <u>characteristic</u> smell of regular household gas.		
a. shared by many	( )	___
b. well-known	( )	___
c. identifying	( )	___

Using Words Precisely (continued)

	Answer	Score

3. Then, the rescuers had to slow down their <u>frenzied</u> digging.

    a. energetic   ( ) ——

    b. wildly excited   ( ) ——

    c. relaxed   ( ) ——

4. They were afraid of loosening <u>debris</u> which would drop onto the trapped students.

    a. pieces of wreckage   ( ) ——

    b. assorted junk   ( ) ——

    c. sound structure   ( ) ——

5. A <u>board</u> <u>of</u> <u>inquiry</u> was set up to sift through the evidence.

    a. team of detectives   ( ) ——

    b. group seeking causes   ( ) ——

    c. group hiding evidence   ( ) ——

Using Words Precisely Score [ ]

B **Choosing the Best Title**

	Answer	Score
Mark the *best title*	(T)	10
Mark the title that is *too broad*	(B)	5
Mark the title that is *too narrow*	(N)	5

	Answer	Score
1. Consolidated School Lacks Central Heating System	( )	——
2. School Explosion	( )	——
3. Gas Causes Fatal School Explosion	( )	——

Choosing the Best Title Score [ ]

C — Recognizing Important Details

	Answer	Score
Mark the details that are *true*	(T)	5
Mark the details that are *false*	(F)	5
Mark the details that are *not mentioned* in the article	(N)	5

	Answer	Score
1. *Wet gas* is safer to burn than regular household gas.	( )	___
2. Most of the younger students had gone home before the explosion.	( )	___
3. The superintendent's own children were in the school when it exploded.	( )	___
4. Many pupils were hurt when the rescuers used heavy wires to pull pieces of wreckage off them.	( )	___
5. All but one of ninety-two seniors survived the explosion.	( )	___
6. *Wet gas* has no color or smell.	( )	___
7. The explosion started in a shop class.	( )	___

Recognizing Important Details Score [ ]

D — Finding the Main Idea

	Answer	Score
Mark the *main idea*	(M)	10
Mark the statement that is *too broad*	(B)	5
Mark the statement that is *too narrow*	(N)	5

	Answer	Score
1. Many oil field people worked to save their own children from the wreckage.	( )	___
2. A tragic explosion occurred at a Texas school.	( )	___
3. A Texas school explosion resulted from using *wet gas* in an effort to reduce heating costs.	( )	___

Finding the Main Idea Score [ ]

A Boeing 747 Jumbo Jet is twice as long as the distance covered by the Wright Brothers during their first flight. It can carry up to 400 passengers. In 1977, *two* jumbo jets collided, killing 580 people in the world's worst air disaster. Here soldiers are working to clear away the wreckage of one of the planes.

19

How Safe Are Those Jumbo Jets?

Read this article well enough so that you can answer questions about it. Your teacher may want you to keep track of your reading time. If so, write your reading time on the SCORECARD on page 129 after you finish the article.

Then answer the questions about the article to find out how well you understood what you read. These questions will help you sharpen your reading and thinking skills.

In the years since the Wright Brothers' first flight, airplanes have grown safer and much larger. The Boeing 747 Jumbo Jet can carry 400 passengers. Although the 747 is one of the world's safest airplanes, there is the possibility of 800 deaths if two of the giant jets should crash into each other. That dreaded crash between two jets became reality in the Canary Islands in 1977.

The Canaries are a group of seven islands in the Atlantic Ocean off the northwest coast of Africa. The islands have belonged to Spain since long before Columbus's first voyage to the New World. As a matter of fact, during that first trip, Columbus stopped at the Canary Islands.

Jumbo jets flying to the Canary Islands usually use the big El Gando Airport. But on Sunday, March 27, 1977, a bomb had gone off at El Gando, so the jumbo jets were diverted to the smaller airport at Tenerife.

Two of the giant 747s detoured to Tenerife were KLM (Dutch Airline) Flight 4805 and Pan American Airways Clipper 1736. The Dutch jet was commanded by Captain Jacob Veldhuizen Van Zanten. Van Zanten, a senior pilot with twenty-five years of flying experience, trained KLM's other pilots. The Pan-Am 747 was captained by Victor Grubbs, a veteran of thirty-two years of flying.

Both aircraft were waiting to take off. The KLM was first in line. The control tower operator ordered the Dutch jet to taxi to the end of the runway using a *taxi strip*, a level piece of ground running along the side of the runway. When the aircraft reached the end of the taxi strip, it would move over onto the runway, ready for take-off. It would then head back down the runway, at top speed, in the direction from which it had started. Partway down the runway, the giant jet would reach flying speed and take off.

The Pan-Am jet taxied down the runway toward the Dutch airplane. The control tower operator planned for the Pan-Am jet to circle to a position behind the KLM 747. Then, a few minutes after the KLM airplane took off, the Pan-Am jumbo would follow. These final maneuvers would take place out of sight of the control tower operator. It was such a foggy day that visibility was limited to a quarter mile, and the runway was almost two miles long.

KLM 4805 had completed its turn and was standing at the end of the runway waiting for the take-off signal from the control tower. At that moment, Pan-Am 1736 was taxiing down the foggy runway straight toward the KLM jet.

The control tower instructed the Dutch jet to stand by. Pan-Am 1736, still taxiing, informed the tower that it would report when it had cleared the runway. The big jet had almost reached the turning off point when somehow, a mixup occurred. The Dutch pilot, who had not been given permission to take off, suddenly started his airplane roaring down the runway.

Aboard the Pan-Am jet, Captain Grubbs and his copilot saw lights cutting through the fog ahead of them. As the glow of the lights grew larger, the pilots realized, to their horror, that an airplane was hurtling down the runway—heading straight for them! Somehow, for some reason, the KLM 747 had started its takeoff.

Grubbs is reported to have shouted, "What's he doing? He'll kill us all!" Then Grubbs desperately gunned his engines and swerved the big 747 in an effort to reach the grass strip along the side of the runway. He succeeded only in presenting the broad side of his aircraft to the Dutch jumbo rushing down the runway at 165 miles per hour.

The Dutch captain finally saw through the fog to the Pan-Am jet in his path. He hauled back on his controls in a desperate effort to take off, or at least to bounce his airplane over the Pan-Am jet. The Dutch airplane did manage to get into the air—but not high enough to clear the Pan-Am plane.

The Dutch 747 plowed into the Pan-Am.

Both of the Pan-Am's wings, all engines still running, collapsed onto the runway. The co-pilot reached for the emergency fire handles over his head. His hand grabbed only air. The entire top of the Pan-Am airplane had been torn off in the crash.

Explosions and fires broke out. The heat was so intense that aluminum and steel parts of both airplanes were vaporized. All 248 people aboard the Dutch jet lost their lives. Of the almost 400 people aboard Pan American Clipper 1736, only 67 survived. It was the worst disaster in the history of air travel.

Could such a freak accident happen again? Anything is possible, but the chances are against it. The airlines' record is so good that the chances of a passenger's reaching a destination safely are 99.999%. Those, any gambler will tell you, are mighty good odds. ∎

Find out your reading time and enter it on the SCORECARD. Then turn to page 157 and look up your reading speed. Write the Words per Minute on the SCORECARD.

Now go on to the exercises in "How Well Did You Read?" Use the SCORE-CARD to record your critical reading scores. When the SCORECARD is full, transfer your Words per Minute and Critical Reading Score to the graphs on pages 158 and 159.

SCORECARD

Reading Speed

Reading Time _____ : _____
Minutes   Seconds

Words per Minute [   ]

How Well Did You Read?

Using Words Precisely _____

Choosing the Best Title _____

Recognizing Important Details _____

Finding the Main Idea _____

Critical Reading Score [   ]
(Add the 4 scores above)

19. How Safe Are Those Jumbo Jets?

How Well Did You Read?

Answer the four types of questions that follow. The directions for each type of question tell you how to mark and score your answers.

After you have answered all the questions, check your work using the Answer Key on page 153. If you have the right answer, write the score on the gray line next to the answer. If your answer is wrong, write 0 on the line.

Then add your scores for each type of question and write the total scores in the gray brackets. Enter the four total scores on the SCORECARD and add them to find your Critical Reading Score.

A Using Words Precisely

	Answer	Score
Mark the word or phrase that has the *same* meaning as the underlined word	(S)	3
Mark the word or phrase that has *almost the same* meaning as the underlined word	(A)	1
Mark the word or phrase that is the *opposite* of the underlined word	(O)	1

	Answer	Score
1. The jumbo jets were <u>diverted</u> to the airport at Tenerife.		
a. transported away	( )	___
b. kept on route	( )	___
c. turned aside	( )	___
2. The control tower operator ordered the Dutch jet to <u>taxi</u> to the end of the runway.		
a. take to the air	( )	___
b. run along the ground	( )	___
c. stay on the ground	( )	___

A — Using Words Precisely (continued)

Answer   Score

3. The Pan-Am 747 was captained by Victor Grubbs, a <u>veteran</u> of thirty-two years of flying.

   a. older person   ( ) ___

   b. experienced person   ( ) ___

   c. new recruit   ( ) ___

4. Then Grubbs desperately <u>gunned</u> his engines and swerved the big 747.

   a. cut the power to   ( ) ___

   b. gave full power to   ( ) ___

   c. sped up   ( ) ___

5. The aluminum and steel parts of both airplanes were <u>vaporized</u>.

   a. heated intensely   ( ) ___

   b. turned to gas   ( ) ___

   c. made more solid   ( ) ___

Using Words Precisely Score [ ]

B — Choosing the Best Title

Answer   Score

Mark the *best title* .... (T) 10

Mark the title that is *too broad* .... (B) 5

Mark the title that is *too narrow* .... (N) 5

Answer   Score

1. Visibility at Airport Limited to ¼ Mile   ( ) ___

2. Jumbo Jets in Accident   ( ) ___

3. 747s Crash at Tenerife   ( ) ___

Choosing the Best Title Score [ ]

C | Recognizing Important Details

	Answer	Score
Mark the details that are *true*	(T)	5
Mark the details that are *false*	(F)	5
Mark the details that are *not mentioned* in the article	(N)	5

	Answer	Score
1. The jets had been detoured to Tenerife because of trouble at another airport.	( )	___
2. The Pan-Am jet was first in line to take off.	( )	___
3. The Pan-Am jet was supposed to come around behind the KLM jet.	( )	___
4. It had been foggy at Tenerife for several days.	( )	___
5. The operator of the control tower gave the instructions in Spanish.	( )	___
6. The first sign of trouble the Pan-Am jet's crew had was the bright lights they saw ahead.	( )	___
7. The Dutch pilot tried to avoid the crash by slamming on the brakes.	( )	___

Recognizing Important Details Score [ ]

D | Finding the Main Idea

	Answer	Score
Mark the *main idea*	(M)	10
Mark the statement that is *too broad*	(B)	5
Mark the statement that is *too narrow*	(N)	5

	Answer	Score
1. Two jumbo jets had a fatal ground collision when one of them started to take off too soon.	( )	___
2. Jets landing at the Canary Islands were diverted to Tenerife because of a bomb explosion.	( )	___
3. Serious aircraft crashes can take place on the ground, as well as in the air.	( )	___

Finding the Main Idea Score [ ]

This scene of a San Francisco street after the earthquake shows
people gazing in amazement at the destruction caused.

20

The San Francisco Earthquake

Read this article well enough so that you can answer questions about it. Your teacher may want you to keep track of your reading time. If so, write your reading time on the SCORECARD on page 135 after you finish the article.

Then answer the questions about the article to find out how well you understood what you read. These questions will help you sharpen your reading and thinking skills.

On April 18, 1906, at 5:12 A.M., San Francisco was rocked by a great earthquake. Although the shock of the quake itself lasted just seconds, it was indirectly responsible for the destruction of three-fourths of the entire city. About 300,000 people were made homeless, and 38,000 buildings were destroyed.

The earthquake itself caused little of this damage. The principal destructive force was the fire caused by the quake. Survivors of the San Francisco disaster have always referred to it, not as "the Earthquake of 1906," but as "the Great Fire of 1906."

San Francisco was a very modern city in 1906, and its modern power system was responsible for its destruction. The shock of the quake broke petroleum tanks and the upheaval of the streets snapped gas mains. All the situation needed to set off a giant conflagration was one spark, and there were sparks aplenty from the broken overhead electric wires. Within seconds, a large part of the city was on fire.

Although the quake claimed relatively few lives, one of the lives it did snuff out was that of the head of the city's fire department. He was crushed when the quake toppled the chimney of his home on top of him.

The fire department was handicapped not only by the tragic loss of its leader, but by the loss of almost all of its water supply. The tremor had snapped the water mains buried deep in the ground. Moreover, the quake had destroyed the city's fire alarm boxes and all telephone communications.

Even if the fire fighters could have received orders, it would have been difficult for them to report to their firehouses since travel, including public transportation, had been brought to a standstill. Train and streetcar lines suffered twisted rails from the upheaval of the streets. During the first few hours after the quake, individual fire fighters and small fire companies could do little more than help extricate victims who were lying helpless, pinned under the wreckage of collapsed buildings.

All civil authorities were as handicapped as the fire department. However, a large military post was located in San Francisco. General Frederick Funston, United States Army, commanded the troops in San Francisco. As a young man Funston had tried to get into West Point but had failed the Military Academy's entrance exam. He enlisted in the army as a private, and his heroism brought him rapid promotion. During service in the Philippine Islands, he won the Congressional Medal of Honor, the highest award the United States gives for valor.

Now, with the city in flames, and the police and fire departments overwhelmed, General Funston took charge. He placed the city under martial law and ordered his troops into the streets. The soldiers carried loaded rifles with bayonets and had orders to "shoot to kill" to prevent looting. Many people had been forced to flee from their homes with only the clothes on their backs. These refugees, in their haste and confusion, had abandoned their homes and valuables, often without even remaining behind long enough to lock their doors. The troops were assigned to protect homes from roving bands of robbers.

The troops' second assignment was to use dynamite and artillery to blow up buildings in the line of the fire's advance. This would create fire-breaks, flat areas in the path of the fire that would halt its advance by denying it any fuel on which it could feed. Some of the fire-breaks did work to slow down the spread of the conflagration. Often, however, before the troops could detonate the dynamite they had planted, the rapidly advancing blaze set it off. The premature explosions hurled flaming wreckage onto buildings not yet touched by the flames. Thus, the dynamiting, rather than retarding the advance of the blaze, sometimes spread it to new areas.

The troops' other mission, the prevention of looting, accomplished a great deal of good, but it also did some harm. The presence of armed soldiers did discourage some would-be looters, but the troops also shot or bayoneted as looters some citizens who were trying to remove their own valuables from their homes before the flames reached them. There is also some evidence that a few soldiers actually became looters themselves, stealing the very property that they were supposed to be guarding.

One section of the city that did not fall victim to either the fire or the dynamiters was the area known as Telegraph Hill. The Italian families who lived there fought the fire block-by-block and house-by-house. They fought with brooms and blankets and buckets of water from San Francisco Bay. And when there was no water, they fought with barrels of home-made red wine from their cellars. They fought—and they won.

Three days after the earthquake, the flames began to come under control. As the blaze approached the waterfront, the city's fire fighters, aided by forces from nearby cities, were able to draw water from San Francisco Bay. Their efforts, combined with the wind's shifting to blow inland from over the water, finally brought the flames under control.

Three-fourths of the city had been destroyed by the quake and the fires that followed. About 700 people had lost their lives, and many of the people who survived felt that they had been touched by God—and spared.

Within five years after the earthquake, San Francisco had been rebuilt and showed no signs of the destruction left by the quake or the fire. Today, a rebuilt San Francisco is the sixth largest city in the United States and the twenty-third largest in the world. ■

Find out your reading time and enter it on the SCORECARD. Then turn to page 157 and look up your reading speed. Write the Words per Minute on the SCORECARD.

Now go on to the exercises in "How Well Did You Read?" Use the SCORE-CARD to record your critical reading scores. When the SCORECARD is full, transfer your Words per Minute and Critical Reading Score to the graphs on pages 158 and 159.

SCORECARD

Reading Speed

Reading Time _____ : _____
Minutes   Seconds

Words per Minute [   ]

How Well Did You Read?

Using Words Precisely ——

Choosing the Best Title ——

Recognizing Important Details ——

Finding the Main Idea ——

Critical Reading Score [   ]
(Add the 4 scores above)

20. The San Francisco Earthquake

How Well Did You Read?

Answer the four types of questions that follow. The directions for each type of question tell you how to mark and score your answers.

After you have answered all the questions, check your work using the Answer Key on page 153. If you have the right answer, write the score on the gray line next to the answer. If your answer is wrong, write 0 on the line.

Then add your scores for each type of question and write the total scores in the gray brackets. Enter the four total scores on the SCORECARD and add them to find your Critical Reading Score.

A Using Words Precisely

	Answer	Score
Mark the word or phrase that has the *same* meaning as the underlined word	(S)	3
Mark the word or phrase that has *almost the same* meaning as the underlined word	(A)	1
Mark the word or phrase that is the *opposite* of the underlined word	(O)	1

	Answer	Score
1. General Funston won high awards for <u>valor</u> in the military service.		
a. boldness	( )	——
b. courage	( )	——
c. cowardice	( )	——
2. Fire companies worked to <u>extricate</u> victims pinned under the wreckage of collapsed buildings.		
a. tie or pin down	( )	——
b. release from a tangle	( )	——
c. help loosen	( )	——

A — Using Words Precisely (continued)

Answer   Score

3. General Funston placed the city under <u>martial</u> law and ordered his troops into the streets.

   a. military ( ) ___

   b. emergency ( ) ___

   c. civilian ( ) ___

4. These <u>refugees</u>, in their haste and confusion, had abandoned their homes and valuables.

   a. people who have left a place ( ) ___

   b. people who seek out danger ( ) ___

   c. people who have fled to safety ( ) ___

5. The dynamiting, rather than <u>retarding</u> the advance of the blaze, sometimes spread it.

   a. slowing down ( ) ___

   b. speeding up ( ) ___

   c. postponing ( ) ___

Using Words Precisely Score [ ]

B — Choosing the Best Title

Answer   Score

Mark the *best title* .... (T)   10

Mark the title that is *too broad* .... (B)   5

Mark the title that is *too narrow* .... (N)   5

Answer   Score

1. The Earthquake That Shook San Francisco ( ) ___

2. Telegraph Hill Families Save Homes From Fire ( ) ___

3. San Francisco, California ( ) ___

Choosing the Best Title Score [ ]

C | Recognizing Important Details

	Answer	Score
Mark the details that are *true*	(T)	5
Mark the details that are *false*	(F)	5
Mark the details that are *not mentioned* in the article	(N)	5

	Answer	Score
1. Trains and streetcars were the only transportation available after the earthquake.	( )	___
2. The fire chief died before he could organize the fire department's work.	( )	___
3. General Funston personally shot several looters.	( )	___
4. Dynamiting buildings sometimes resulted in spreading the fire.	( )	___
5. The Italian families on Telegraph Hill lost their homes to the fire when they ran out of water and wine to fight it.	( )	___
6. Nearby cities, fearing a second quake, refused to send their fire fighters to San Francisco.	( )	___
7. The quake and the fire left about 300,000 people homeless.	( )	___

Recognizing Important Details Score [ ]

D | Finding the Main Idea

	Answer	Score
Mark the *main idea*	(M)	10
Mark the statement that is *too broad*	(B)	5
Mark the statement that is *too narrow*	(N)	5

	Answer	Score
1. The San Francisco earthquake and fire were destructive.	( )	___
2. Fires started from electric and gas lines broken by the San Francisco earthquake.	( )	___
3. The fire caused by the San Francisco earthquake was even more destructive than the tremor.	( )	___

Finding the Main Idea Score [ ]

21

Unscheduled Stop on the Long Island Railroad

Read this article well enough so that you can answer questions about it. Your teacher may want you to keep track of your reading time. If so, write your reading time on the SCORECARD on page 141 after you finish the article.

Then answer the questions about the article to find out how well you understood what you read. These questions will help you sharpen your reading and thinking skills.

The Long Island Railroad is the busiest commuter line in the United States, providing transportation for the people who live in the bedroom communities surrounding New York City. Every day, these commuters ride from 25 to 200 miles back and forth between their homes on Long Island and their places of work in the city.

On the day before Thanksgiving, 1950, the railroad was even busier than usual. Thousands of commuters had jammed New York City's Pennsylvania Station all day. By 6:09 P.M. when the eastbound train going to Hempstead, Long Island, pulled out, however, the crowd of pre-holiday travelers had lessened to the point

where there were seats enough for all its 1,000 passengers. A few minutes later, the 6:13 Express for Babylon followed the earlier train eastward. It carried 1,200 passengers. Both trains were self-contained: each was pulled by a motor in its first passenger car. For the first part of the trip, both trains would travel on the same track. The first stop for both was to have been Jamaica, a station at the eastern end of New York City. 2,200 people would be traveling aboard two trains that shared the same track, with only a four-minute gap between them.

In Queens, New York City, the track ran along the top of a fifteen-foot-high embankment, and, ordinarily, the 6:09 train would have run right on through this section of track without stopping. This evening, however, the 6:09 had to stop for a red light. When the signal turned green again, Engineer William Murphy, a thirty-one-year railroad veteran, started up the engine and proceeded. Then, the brakes grabbed, bringing the train to a second, completely unexpected halt.

The rules of the railroad required that the crew of a train making an unscheduled stop set out red lanterns on the track

behind the train. If another train were following close behind, flares or torpedoes had to be used in addition to the red lanterns. The torpedoes, placed on the track, would go off with a loud bang when the second train ran over them, thus signaling the train's engineer of danger ahead. Flagman Bertram Biggan had run back down the tracks from the lead car when the train had stopped for the red light, and had put a red lantern behind the last car. As Biggan had been about to light flares, he had heard the engine of his train start up again. The flagman had run back to the train to avoid being left behind. He hadn't had time to place flares or torpedoes. Then, the brakes grabbed and the train halted for a second time with no flares or torpedoes on the track.

One thousand passengers sat aboard the stalled 6:09 as the 6:13 bore down on them.

The 6:13 Express was coming down the track, driven by Engineer Benjamin Pokorney, a thirty-one-year veteran like his colleague, William Murphy. Pokorney's eyes were fixed, not on the track itself, but on the overhead system of signal lights. He saw the green light that had just flashed the go-ahead signal not

The Long Island Railroad often runs late, but it has one of the most modern signal systems in the world. But in 1950, the signal system failed to prevent a tragic accident. The 6:13 Express to Babylon, Long Island, plowed into the rear of an earlier train, telescoping cars and killing seventy-nine people.

for his train, but for the earlier train.

The 6:13 continued at forty miles an hour and plowed into the rear of the 6:09!

Fred Mergi was a passenger aboard the last car of the stalled 6:09. He had been watching as Flagman Biggan placed the red lantern behind the stalled train and then climbed back aboard. Suddenly, Mergi saw a blinking flash of white light— the headlight of the approaching 6:13. He threw himself on the floor of the aisle a split second before the 6:13 plowed into the last car of the 6:09, lifting its back end into the air. Mergi slid down the aisle of his car as the onrushing 6:13 passed through the inside of the 6:09. Mergi lived, but most of the other passengers weren't so lucky.

There was a crash of shattering glass and the terrible screech of metal ground against metal—and against human bodies, too. People were decapitated, heads going one way, bodies going the other way. The first part of the 6:13 pierced the back of the 6:09. It was as if some evil, giant hand had telescoped one car into the other. The first car of the second train simply tore through the last car of the first train, compressing and ripping apart seats and the people sitting

on them. Most of the casualties were in those two cars: there were 79 dead, and 318 injured. The accident was the worst rail disaster of modern times, and one of the worst in railroading history.

The crash occurred in Richmond Hill, a residential section of New York City. The people there were just sitting down to dinner when they heard a noise many thought was caused by an atomic bomb. They rushed from their homes and ran up the fifteen-foot embankment. One of the horrors that greeted them was the sight of passengers still seated in the train, their sightless eyes gazing out of the windows. Other passengers, trapped in the tangled metal wreckage, cried for help.

Soon a crowd of more than 5,000 had gathered. Neighborhood people carried the injured into homes that had been turned into emergency medical centers. The passengers who were not badly wounded were given hot coffee, tea and soup. Medics arrived from several New York City and Long Island hospitals, and doctors moved among the injured, giving first aid and administering morphine. They worked far into the cold November night, wearing blankets over their white hospital uniforms.

Two interns from nearby Queens General Hospital, Dr. Paul Soffer and Dr. Arnold Sanders, climbed into the telescoped cars through the windows. They worked non-stop for five hours, helping passengers trapped in the cramped spaces. Then, the last patient cared for, the two doctors wriggled out of the wreck—and collapsed from exhaustion.

Floodlights, hastily set up, etched the scenes of disaster against the black night. Acetylene torches added their flickering light. Soon, a wrecking train with huge cranes arrived to separate the railroad cars. By dawn, all the dead and wounded had been cared for, and the only evidence of the disaster that remained was a bandage lying near the track and a baby blanket hanging from a fence.

The nation was horrified at news reports of the disaster. One well-meaning person felt there was a way of preventing similar tragedies in the future. "I notice," this person wrote to a Long Island newspaper, "that in train accidents it's the passengers in the first and last cars who get hurt. Why don't they run trains that don't have first and last cars?" ■

Find out your reading time and enter it on the SCORECARD. Then turn to page 157 and look up your reading speed. Write the Words per Minute on the SCORECARD.

Now go on to the exercises in "How Well Did You Read?" Use the SCORECARD to record your critical reading scores. When the SCORECARD is full, transfer your Words per Minute and Critical Reading Score to the graphs on pages 158 and 159.

SCORECARD

Reading Speed

Reading Time _____ : _____
Minutes   Seconds

Words per Minute [   ]

How Well Did You Read?

Using Words Precisely _____

Choosing the Best Title _____

Recognizing Important Details _____

Finding the Main Idea _____

Critical Reading Score [   ]
(Add the 4 scores above)

21. Unscheduled Stop on the Long Island Railroad

How Well Did You Read?

Answer the four types of questions that follow. The directions for each type of question tell you how to mark and score your answers.

After you have answered all the questions, check your work using the Answer Key on page 153. If you have the right answer, write the score on the gray line next to the answer. If your answer is wrong, write 0 on the line.

Then add your scores for each type of question and write the total scores in the gray brackets. Enter the four total scores on the SCORECARD and add them to find your Critical Reading Score.

A Using Words Precisely

	Answer	Score
Mark the word or phrase that has the *same* meaning as the underlined word	(S)	3
Mark the word or phrase that has *almost the same* meaning as the underlined word	(A)	1
Mark the word or phrase that is the *opposite* of the underlined word	(O)	1

	Answer	Score
1. The Long Island Railroad is the busiest <u>commuter</u> line in the United States.		
a. person who travels as a tourist	( )	___
b. person who travels to work	( )	___
c. person who works at home	( )	___
2. Medics moved among the injured, <u>administering</u> morphine.		
a. taking away	( )	___
b. giving out	( )	___
c. delivering	( )	___

A   Using Words Precisely (continued)

Answer   Score

3. People were <u>decapitated</u>, heads going one way, bodies going the other way.

    a. having head injuries   ( ) ____

    b. left whole   ( ) ____

    c. beheaded   ( ) ____

4. The first car tore through the last car, <u>compressing</u> seats.

    a. squeezing together   ( ) ____

    b. pressing against   ( ) ____

    c. letting loose   ( ) ____

5. The doctors climbed into the <u>telescoped</u> cars through the windows.

    a. fitted one inside the other   ( ) ____

    b. pulled out to their full lengths   ( ) ____

    c. forced together, one inside the other   ( ) ____

Using Words Precisely Score   [ ]

B   Choosing the Best Title

Answer   Score

Mark the *best title* .... (T)   10

Mark the title that is *too broad* .... (B)   5

Mark the title that is *too narrow* .... (N)   5

Answer   Score

1. Babylon Express Hits Hempstead Train   ( ) ____

2. U.S. Railroad Accident   ( ) ____

3. New York City Railroad Crash   ( ) ____

Choosing the Best Title Score   [ ]

C — Recognizing Important Details

	Answer	Score
Mark the details that are *true*	(T)	5
Mark the details that are *false*	(F)	5
Mark the details that are *not mentioned* in the article	(N)	5

	Answer	Score
1. Many passengers intended to stay overnight in Hempstead for Thanksgiving dinners.	( )	___
2. The worst injuries occurred to passengers in two of the railroad cars.	( )	___
3. The 6:09 train had stopped for a short time, started up, then stopped again.	( )	___
4. The engineers of both trains had perfect safety records up to the time of the Richmond Hill crash.	( )	___
5. Both engineers had the same number of years of railroad experience.	( )	___
6. Passenger Fred Mergi tried to stop the express with a red lantern.	( )	___
7. It took several days to clear the wreckage from the tracks at Richmond Hill.	( )	___

Recognizing Important Details Score [ ]

D — Finding the Main Idea

	Answer	Score
Mark the *main idea*	(M)	10
Mark the statement that is *too broad*	(B)	5
Mark the statement that is *too narrow*	(N)	5

	Answer	Score
1. Many casualties resulted when a Long Island Railroad express ran into a stalled train.	( )	___
2. Two Long Island Railroad trains collided on the way out to Long Island.	( )	___
3. A total of 79 people were killed in the Richmond Hill section of Queens, New York City.	( )	___

Finding the Main Idea Score [ ]

Answer Key

Answer Key

1. Bad Good Friday in Anchorage

A. Using Words Precisely
1. a. O b. A c. S   4. a. A b. O c. S
2. a. O b. A c. S   5. a. S b. O c. A
3. a. A b. S c. O

B. Choosing the Best Title
1. B
2. T
3. N

C. Recognizing Important Details
1. F   5. F
2. F   6. T
3. T   7. N
4. N

D. Finding the Main Idea
1. M
2. N
3. B

2. The Tornado That Ripped St. Louis Apart

A. Using Words Precisely
1. a. A b. S c. O   4. a. O b. S c. A
2. a. O b. A c. S   5. a. A b. S c. O
3. a. S b. O c. A

B. Choosing the Best Title
1. N
2. B
3. T

C. Recognizing Important Details
1. T   5. T
2. F   6. N
3. F   7. T
4. F

D. Finding the Main Idea
1. B
2. M
3. N

3. Fire on the High Seas

A. Using Words Precisely
1. a. O b. S c. A   4. a. A b. S c. O
2. a. S b. A c. O   5. a. A b. S c. O
3. a. O b. A c. S

B. Choosing the Best Title
1. N
2. B
3. T

C. Recognizing Important Details
1. F   5. T
2. T   6. T
3. N   7. F
4. T

D. Finding the Main Idea
1. B
2. M
3. N

4. Pompeii: The City That Slept for 1500 Years

A. Using Words Precisely

1. a. O b. S c. A   4. a. S b. O c. A
2. a. A b. S c. O   5. a. A b. O c. S
3. a. A b. S c. O

B. Choosing the Best Title

1. N
2. T
3. B

C. Recognizing Important Details

1. F   5. T
2. F   6. F
3. N   7. F
4. T

D. Finding the Main Idea

1. B
2. N
3. M

5. Monongah Mine Explosion Traps 368

A. Using Words Precisely

1. a. A b. S c. O   4. a. O b. S c. A
2. a. S b. A c. O   5. a. S b. O c. A
3. a. O b. A c. S

B. Choosing the Best Title

1. N
2. B
3. T

C. Recognizing Important Details

1. T   5. N
2. F   6. N
3. F   7. T
4. F

D. Finding the Main Idea

1. N
2. B
3. M

6. The *Hindenburg*: Last of the Great Dirigibles

A. Using Words Precisely

1. a. A b. S c. O   4. a. O b. S c. A
2. a. O b. A c. S   5. a. A b. O c. S
3. a. O b. A c. S

B. Choosing the Best Title

1. B
2. T
3. N

C. Recognizing Important Details

1. T   5. F
2. F   6. N
3. N   7. F
4. T

D. Finding the Main Idea

1. M
2. B
3. N

7. Take to the Hills! The Johnstown Dam is Going!

A. Using Words Precisely
1. a. A b. S c. O   4. a. O b. A c. S
2. a. O b. A c. S   5. a. A b. O c. S
3. a. S b. A c. O

B. Choosing the Best Title
1. B
2. T
3. N

C. Recognizing Important Details
1. T   5. T
2. N   6. T
3. F   7. F
4. N

D. Finding the Main Idea
1. N
2. M
3. B

8. Death of the Unsinkable *Titanic*

A. Using Words Precisely
1. a. O b. A c. S   4. a. O b. S c. A
2. a. S b. A c. O   5. a. S b. O c. A
3. a. A b. S c. O

B. Choosing the Best Title
1. T
2. N
3. B

C. Recognizing Important Details
1. T   5. T
2. F   6. F
3. N   7. F
4. N

D. Finding the Main Idea
1. B
2. M
3. N

9. Galveston: The City That Drowned

A. Using Words Precisely
1. a. S b. A c. O   4. a. A b. S c. O
2. a. O b. S c. A   5. a. A b. O c. S
3. a. S b. O c. A

B. Choosing the Best Title
1. N
2. T
3. B

C. Recognizing Important Details
1. T   5. F
2. T   6. N
3. F   7. F
4. N

D. Finding the Main Idea
1. B
2. M
3. N

10. Boston's Cocoanut Grove Ablaze

A. Using Words Precisely
1. a. A b. S c. O   4. a. A b. S c. O
2. a. O b. A c. S   5. a. S b. O c. A
3. a. O b. S c. A

B. Choosing the Best Title
1. B
2. T
3. N

C. Recognizing Important Details
1. T   5. F
2. T   6. T
3. N   7. N
4. F

D. Finding the Main Idea
1. B
2. N
3. M

11. Krakatoa: The Doomsday Crack Heard 'Round the World

A. Using Words Precisely
1. a. S b. A c. O   4. a. O b. A c. S
2. a. O b. S c. A   5. a. A b. S c. O
3. a. A b. O c. S

B. Choosing the Best Title
1. N
2. B
3. T

C. Recognizing Important Details
1. N   5. T
2. T   6. N
3. F   7. F
4. T

D. Finding the Main Idea
1. M
2. B
3. N

12. Halifax: City Blown to Pieces

A. Using Words Precisely
1. a. S b. O c. A   4. a. S b. A c. O
2. a. A b. S c. O   5. a. A b. O c. S
3. a. O b. A c. S

B. Choosing the Best Title
1. N
2. B
3. T

C. Recognizing Important Details
1. T   5. F
2. N   6. T
3. F   7. T
4. N

D. Finding the Main Idea
1. B
2. M
3. N

13. Terror in the Fog

A. Using Words Precisely
1. a. O b. A c. S   4. a. S b. O c. A
2. a. S b. A c. O   5. a. S b. O c. A
3. a. A b. S c. O

B. Choosing the Best Title
1. B
2. N
3. T

C. Recognizing Important Details
1. N   5. T
2. F   6. N
3. N   7. T
4. T

D. Finding the Main Idea
1. N
2. B
3. M

14. The Circus Troupe's Last Performance

A. Using Words Precisely
1. a. S b. O c. A   4. a. O b. S c. A
2. a. A b. S c. O   5. a. A b. S c. O
3. a. O b. A c. S

B. Choosing the Best Title
1. T
2. B
3. N

C. Recognizing Important Details
1. F   5. F
2. N   6. F
3. T   7. F
4. T

D. Finding the Main Idea
1. B
2. N
3. M

15. Black Death: The End of the World

A. Using Words Precisely
1. a. O b. A c. S   4. a. S b. O c. A
2. a. A b. S c. O   5. a. O b. A c. S
3. a. S b. O c. A

B. Choosing the Best Title
1. B
2. N
3. T

C. Recognizing Important Details
1. T   5. T
2. F   6. F
3. N   7. T
4. N

D. Finding the Main Idea
1. B
2. M
3. N

16. The Great Chicago Fire

A. Using Words Precisely
1. a. S b. A c. O   4. a. A b. O c. S
2. a. S b. A c. O   5. a. S b. A c. O
3. a. O b. A c. S

B. Choosing the Best Title
1. N
2. B
3. T

C. Recognizing Important Details
1. F   5. T
2. F   6. N
3. T   7. T
4. F

D. Finding the Main Idea
1. B
2. M
3. N

17. The Sinking of the *Lusitania*

A. Using Words Precisely
1. a. O b. A c. S   4. a. S b. A c. O
2. a. A b. S c. O   5. a. S b. A c. O
3. a. A b. S c. O

B. Choosing the Best Title
1. B
2. T
3. N

C. Recognizing Important Details
1. F   5. F
2. N   6. T
3. F   7. T
4. T

D. Finding the Main Idea
1. B
2. M
3. N

18. Penny-Pinching Brings Death at the World's Richest School

A. Using Words Precisely
1. a. O b. A c. S   4. a. S b. A c. O
2. a. O b. A c. S   5. a. A b. S c. O
3. a. A b. S c. O

B. Choosing the Best Title
1. N
2. B
3. T

C. Recognizing Important Details
1. F   5. F
2. T   6. T
3. N   7. T
4. N

D. Finding the Main Idea
1. N
2. B
3. M

19. How Safe Are Those Jumbo Jets?

A. Using Words Precisely

1. a. A   b. O   c. S   4. a. O   b. S   c. A
2. a. O   b. S   c. A   5. a. A   b. S   c. O
3. a. A   b. S   c. O

B. Choosing the Best Title

1. N
2. B
3. T

C. Recognizing Important Details

1. T   5. N
2. F   6. T
3. T   7. F
4. N

D. Finding the Main Idea

1. M
2. N
3. B

20. The San Francisco Earthquake

A. Using Words Precisely

1. a. A   b. S   c. O   4. a. A   b. O   c. S
2. a. O   b. S   c. A   5. a. S   b. O   c. A
3. a. S   b. A   c. O

B. Choosing the Best Title

1. T
2. N
3. B

C. Recognizing Important Details

1. F   5. F
2. F   6. N
3. N   7. T
4. T

D. Finding the Main Idea

1. B
2. N
3. M

21. Unscheduled Stop on the Long Island Railroad

A. Using Words Precisely

1. a. A   b. S   c. O   4. a. S   b. A   c. O
2. a. O   b. S   c. A   5. a. A   b. O   c. S
3. a. A   b. O   c. S

B. Choosing the Best Title

1. N
2. B
3. T

C. Recognizing Important Details

1. N   5. T
2. T   6. F
3. T   7. F
4. N

D. Finding the Main Idea

1. M
2. B
3. N

Words per Minute Table
& Progress Graphs

Minutes and Seconds	1. Bad Good Friday	2. St. Louis Tornado	3. Fire on the High Seas	4. Pompeii	5. Monongah Mine Explosion	6. The *Hindenburg*	7. Johnstown Dam	8. Death of the *Titanic*	9. Galveston	10. Boston's Cocoanut Grove	11. Krakatoa	Seconds
1:00	867	782	1018	857	758	937	1108	1064	806	926	801	60
1:15	694	626	814	686	606	750	886	851	645	741	640	75
1:30	578	521	679	571	505	625	739	709	537	617	534	90
1:45	495	447	582	490	433	535	633	608	461	529	458	105
2:00	434	391	509	429	379	469	554	532	403	463	401	120
2:15	385	348	452	381	337	416	494	473	358	412	356	135
2:30	347	313	407	343	303	375	443	426	322	370	320	150
2:45	315	284	370	312	276	341	403	387	293	337	291	165
3:00	289	261	339	286	253	312	369	355	269	309	267	180
3:15	267	241	313	264	233	288	341	327	248	285	246	195
3:30	248	223	291	245	217	268	317	304	230	265	229	210
3:45	231	209	271	229	202	250	295	284	215	247	214	225
4:00	217	196	255	214	190	234	277	266	202	232	200	240
4:15	204	184	240	202	178	220	261	250	190	218	188	255
4:30	193	174	226	190	168	208	246	236	179	206	178	270
4:45	183	165	214	180	160	197	233	224	170	195	169	285
5:00	173	156	204	171	152	187	222	213	161	185	160	300
5:30	158	142	185	156	138	170	201	193	147	168	146	330
6:00	145	130	170	143	126	156	185	177	134	154	134	360
6:30	133	120	157	132	117	144	170	164	124	142	123	390
7:00	124	112	145	122	108	134	158	152	115	132	114	420
7:30	116	104	136	114	101	125	148	142	107	123	107	450
8:00	108	98	127	107	95	117	138	133	101	116	100	480
8:30	102	92	120	101	89	110	130	125	95	109	94	510

Minutes and Seconds	12. Halifax	13. Terror in the Fog	14. Circus Troupe	15. Black Death	16. Great Chicago Fire	17. Sinking of the Lusitania	18. World's Richest School	19. Jumbo Jets	20. San Francisco Earthquake	21. Unscheduled Stop	Seconds
1:00	839	975	934	1068	1167	1010	807	859	958	1142	60
1:15	671	780	747	854	934	808	646	687	766	914	75
1:30	559	650	623	712	778	673	538	573	639	761	90
1:45	479	557	534	610	667	577	461	491	547	653	105
2:00	420	488	467	534	584	505	404	430	479	571	120
2:15	373	433	415	475	519	449	359	382	426	508	135
2:30	336	390	374	427	467	404	323	344	383	457	150
2:45	305	355	340	388	424	367	293	312	348	415	165
3:00	280	325	311	356	389	337	269	286	319	381	180
3:15	258	300	287	329	359	311	248	264	295	351	195
3:30	240	279	267	305	333	289	231	245	274	326	210
3:45	224	260	249	285	311	269	215	229	255	305	225
4:00	210	244	234	267	292	253	202	215	240	286	240
4:15	197	229	220	251	275	238	190	202	225	269	255
4:30	186	217	208	237	259	224	179	191	213	254	270
4:45	177	205	197	225	246	213	170	181	202	240	285
5:00	168	195	187	214	233	202	161	172	192	228	300
5:30	153	177	170	194	212	184	147	156	174	208	330
6:00	140	163	156	178	195	168	135	143	160	190	360
6:30	129	150	144	164	180	155	124	132	147	176	390
7:00	120	139	133	153	167	144	115	123	137	163	420
7:30	112	130	125	142	156	135	108	115	128	152	450
8:00	105	122	117	134	146	126	101	107	120	143	480
8:30	99	115	110	126	137	119	95	101	113	134	510

How Well Did You Read?

Directions: *Write your Critical Reading Score in the box under the number for each unit. Then put an* **x** *along the line above each box to show your Critical Reading Score for that unit. Make a graph of your progress by drawing a line to connect the* **x**'s.

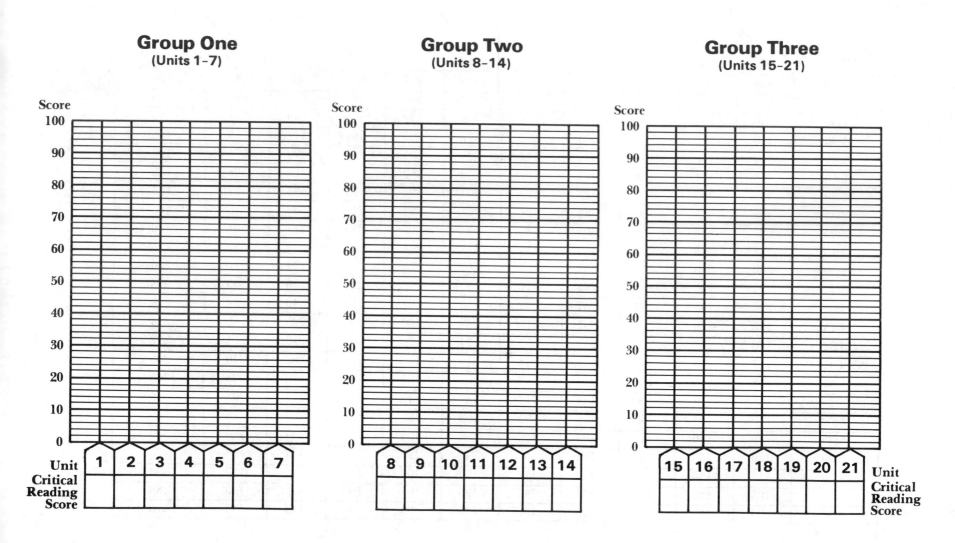

Group One
(Units 1–7)

Group Two
(Units 8–14)

Group Three
(Units 15–21)

Reading Speed

Directions: *Write your Words per Minute score in the box under the number for each unit.*
*Then put an **x** along the line above each box to show your reading speed for that unit.*
*Make a graph of your progress by drawing a line to connect the **x**'s.*

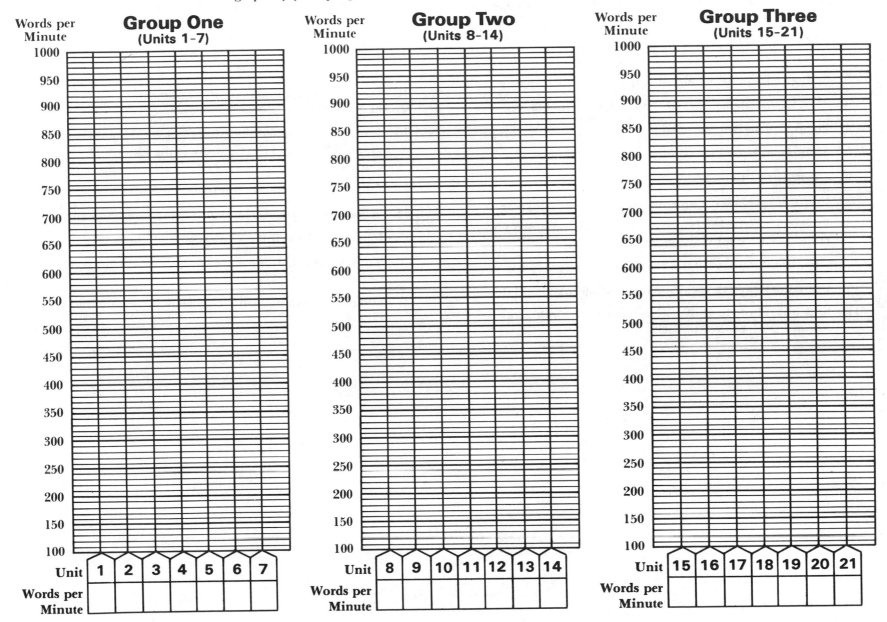

Photo and Picture Credits

Cover: Mayon volcano ejects molten lava and rocks, Legaspi City, Philippines. UPI/Bettmann Newsphotos

1. Anchorage Earthquake: United Press International Telephoto

2. St. Louis Tornado: Courtesy of the Library of Congress

3. *Morro Castle:* Acme, United Press International Photo

4. Pompeii: The Bettmann Archive

5. Monongah Mine Explosion: Wide World Photos

6. *Hindenburg:* United Press International Photo

7. Johnstown Flood: Courtesy of the Library of Congress

8. *Titanic:* United Press International Photo; *Alvin:* Woods Hole Oceanographic Institution

9. Galveston: Courtesy of the Library of Congress

10. Cocoanut Grove: Acme, United Press International Photo

11. Krakatoa: Photo by R. W. Decker, *Journal of Geophysical Research* (Vol. 66, No. 10, 1960)

12. Halifax Harbor: United Press International Photo

13. Empire State Building Crash: United Press International Photo

14. Circus Train: Chicago Historical Society

15. Black Death: National Library of Medicine, Bethesda, Maryland 20014

16. Chicago Fire: United Press International Photo; Lithograph, The Great Fire: Courtesy of the Library of Congress

17. *Lusitania:* United Press International Photo

18. School Explosion: Acme, United Press International Photo

19. Jumbo Jets: United Press International Photo

20. San Francisco Earthquake: Courtesy of the Library of Congress

21. Long Island Train Crash: Acme, United Press International Photo